BEN JONSON

THE ALCHEMIST

BEN JONSON

THE ALCHEMIST

Edited by

R. J. L. KINGSFORD, M.A.
Late Scholar of Clare College, Cambridge

===

CAMBRIDGE
AT THE UNIVERSITY PRESS
1962

PUBLISHED BY
THE SYNDICS OF THE CAMBRIDGE UNIVERSITY PRESS

Bentley House, 200 Euston Road, London, N.W. 1
American Branch: 32 East 57th Street, New York 22, N.Y.
West African Office: P.O. Box 33, Ibadan, Nigeria

First Edition 1928
Reprinted 1936
1941
1946 (*twice*)
1948
1952
1958
1962

Printed in Great Britain at the University Press, Cambridge
(*Brooke Crutchley, University Printer*)

CONTENTS

¶ Except that the spelling and
punctuation have been occasionally
modernised and a few passages
omitted, the text of William Gifford's
edition of 1816 has been followed.

INTRODUCTION

BEN JONSON was born in Westminster in 1573; and with a few short breaks he lived the whole of his life in the London which is so vividly reflected in *The Alchemist*. His father, a minister, died a month before he was born, and two years later his mother re-married. Her second husband, who was a bricklayer, may have had little sympathy with his step-son's scholarly leanings, but at any rate he deserves our gratitude for making good provision for his education by sending him to Westminster School. On leaving Westminster, Jonson himself tells us that he was put to a trade, which we may assume to have been that of a bricklayer, but this suited him ill and before long we find him soldiering in the Low Countries. We know that he was married not later than 1592 and that by 1597 he had begun his connection with the stage, as an actor under Henslowe's management. One of the most popular plays of the period was *The Spanish Tragedy* by Thomas Kyd, and we can picture Jonson taking the very part of Jeronimo to which we shall find him referring in *The Alchemist*. In 1598 he produced his first important comedy, *Every Man in his Humour*, in which a part was played by no less a person than William Shakespeare. In the same year Jonson's career suffered a short set-back which might well have turned out more seriously. In a quarrel he killed another member of Henslowe's company, Gabriel Spenser, and was imprisoned for murder. His release was, fortunately, procured after a few months, but in the meantime, as a result of visits received from a priest, Jonson had become a Roman Catholic. After his release his plays follow one another in quick succession, the most notable being *Every Man out of his Humour* (1599) and his first tragedy, *Sejanus* (1603). The accession of James I, who was himself a man of letters, and a patron of literature accordingly, was a fortunate event for Jonson no less than for others of his profession; and in the early years of the reign he found plenty of employment in writing masques for the entertainment of the Court. In these years his success was at its height and by 1616 he had produced nearly all the plays upon which his reputation rests, including *Volpone, or the Fox* (1605), his two masterpieces, *Epicoene, or the Silent Woman* (1609) and *The Alchemist* (1610), and his second tragedy *Catiline* (1611). The remaining years of Jonson's life are of little moment. In 1616 he received a pension of 100 marks a year, a sum which seems to have fluctuated from time to time. In 1618 he took a holiday from the drama and spent a year and a half in Scotland, staying for part of the time with William Drummond of Hawthornden, who has left us a delightful legacy of *Conversations* with Ben Jonson. Much, also, of his leisure in London during this period was spent in conversation within the circle of literary men who gathered at the Mermaid Tavern. The accession of Charles I marks the beginning of the final period of his career, in which, forced to supplement his pension and his salary as city chronologer, he took to writing for the stage again; but he produced no more great comedies—and it is with this, the most important, branch of his genius that we are here concerned. He died in 1637.

Jonson's comedies are essentially a part of his own time; and of all his plays *The Alchemist* most reflects the Jacobean London in which he lived. Not only is it full of contemporary allusions, to the new Royal Exchange and the commerce to which Elizabeth's reign had given such an impetus, to the money-lenders and other swindlers with which London swarmed, to the new and fashionable pastime of smoking, and so forth; but its very plot hinges upon an actual event of the year in which the play was written and produced: the plague which visited London during the summer of 1610. Frightened by the plague,

Lovewit quits the city and leaves his house in the charge of his servant Jeremy, who under the assumed name of Face enters into an 'indenture tripartite' with Subtle, a professional alchemist, and Dol Common, to practise alchemy and any other profitable form of swindling that may present itself. The lure of the promised gold draws to them a succession of dupes. Mammon, the knight, hopes to have all the metal in his house transmuted into gold and to rise to unparalleled heights of riches and luxury. The Puritans, Ananias and Tribulation Wholesome, propose by hiring soldiers and bribing magistrates, to establish Puritanism firmly in England. Dapper, a lawyer's clerk, seeks a familiar spirit to advise him in his gambling. Drugger, a tobacconist, demands a magic sign to draw custom to his shop and directions for the placing of his shelves in the most fortunate position. Kastril is taught how to be a fashionable town 'blood'; and his sister, Widow Pliant, is told her fortune in marriage. Each in turn is robbed of his goods and his money; and the swindlers' success is complete, until the unexpected return of Face's master sees the discomfiture of all, with the exception of Face himself. Even from this skeleton of the play it can be seen how much the action is interwoven with everyday events of Jonson's time; he had, in fact, a plot which provided him with exceptional opportunities for satirising two social pests of the age: Puritanism and the profession of alchemy.

The theory of alchemy is difficult to describe in any but a vague way, for it was the outcome of vague thinking. The alchemists' theory that they could turn any metal into gold rested upon one fundamental belief: that every substance of nature has an essential principle or element out of which it has grown, as a chicken grows out of an egg, and that, further, there is an element common to all these essential principles—a universal essence. Thus they believed that, since there is a property common to all substances, firstly one substance could be turned into another and secondly an imperfect substance could be developed into a perfect one, if only by their art the

fundamental essence could be fostered and increased.
As Subtle himself is made to say:

> '"Twere absurd
> To think that nature in the earth bred gold
> Perfect in the instant: something went before.
> There must be remote matter.'

To find this 'remote matter' in every substance and to
distil the one perfect element common to all was the
alchemists' aim; and the elixir they sought they called
'the philosopher's stone.' This once discovered, all nature
would be at their command. The growth of the quintessence could be quickened by their art, the imperfect could
be made perfect, the most worthless metal turned to gold,
by the application of the philosopher's stone. The general
was however ignored for the particular; and the end of
alchemy was soon taken to be, not the extraction of the
quintessence of all things, but the making of gold and
silver. The 'remote matter' they believed to be partly
a liquid, partly a solid, substance, which, mixed together,
formed stones and metals; the preponderance of the solid
producing stones, the preponderance of the liquid producing quicksilver and sulphur, the parents of all metals.
The philosopher's stone itself was apparently conceived
to consist of the elements of seven metals (each of them
called by the name of a celestial body: gold being the
sun, silver the moon, iron Mars and so forth) of which
quicksilver, or mercury, was the most important, and of
the elements of four spirits, sulphur being the most
important of these. These metals and spirits, properly
distilled and mixed, formed the 'stone.' Of these vague
speculations no better description could be found than
that which Jonson himself puts into the mouth of Subtle
(see pp. 32–34); indeed, Jonson puts the case for alchemy
as fairly and plausibly as could a professor of that art.

Popular belief in alchemy and the following of it as a
profession have fluctuated considerably. In the Middle
Ages it was generally believed in and the names of many
scholars, including Paracelsus, can be counted among its

adherents. In England in the reign of Edward III we find the craft of multiplying gold and silver recognised at the Mint and by the end of the fourteenth century it had become of sufficient public importance to be satirised by Chaucer in his *Canon's Yeoman's Tale* and to be declared a felony by a statute of 1403. Little is heard of alchemy in the early part of the fifteenth century, but by 1450 it was at its zenith and Henry VI instituted commissions to enquire into it as a means of replenishing his treasury. The practice declined again in the following century, but in Queen Elizabeth's reign the country was alive with alchemists, the cause being no doubt supported by the fact that the Queen herself was a believer; and hand in hand with the alchemists went the astrologers, palmists and other dealers in magic. This was the state of affairs which Jonson found in 1610; and in drawing the characters of Subtle and Face there can be little doubt that he had in mind three well-known names of the period, John Dee and Simon Forman, to both of whom Subtle bears some resemblance, and Edward Kelley, the prototype of Face. Dee, who appears to have been a sincere believer in alchemy, was a mathematician and an astronomer of repute, who in his later years interested himself in alchemy and magic in general and associated himself with Kelley. Kelley, a clever charlatan, obtained a complete mastery over him and together they toured the Continent, holding *séances* with spirits and transmuting metals. In particular they spent much time with Albert Laski, a Polish nobleman, and Rudolph II, Emperor of Germany, who eventually detained Kelley in prison. To their partnership the alliance of Subtle and Face bears a resemblance, for both Kelley and Face frequently trick and outwit their partners. The career of Forman must have provided Jonson with even better material. He was the best-known quack of the time and, like Subtle, had an extensive practice in London not only in alchemy, but in medicine, necromancy, astrology and crystal-gazing.

Alchemy and its allied sciences form the basis of Jonson's plot. The Puritans, the other of the two social

pests which he satirises, he treats more incidentally but
with even more contempt for their hypocrisy. The current
objections to the Puritans and their jargon, probably
somewhat exaggerated, will be found enumerated by
Jonson in Act III, Scene 2 (pp. 51, 52). The quarrel
between them and the stage was of long standing. The
Puritans attacked the stage in general; the stage returned
the attack and got the better of the argument. Contemporary drama abounded in references to the Puritans,
until in 1642 the theatres were closed by Act of Parlia-
ment. To Jonson's scholarly mind the comic possibilities
of an argument between the Puritan jargon and the
jargon of alchemy offered an obvious appeal.

Jonson was the most scholarly of the Elizabethan
dramatists. It was the scholar in him which made him
put into Subtle's mouth something more than the usual
jargon of a swindling alchemist and made him give him
as erudite a case as a confirmed adherent of alchemy
could have put forward. It was to the scholar in him that
the pseudo-science of alchemy appealed as an object of
ridicule. It was, too, his classical training which made
him realise that Elizabethan drama obeyed no rules; and
he, therefore, attempted to conform to the theory, first
laid down by Aristotle, that drama should have 'unity'
of action and, the natural deduction from Aristotle's
theory, that the imagination and 'willing suspension
of disbelief' required in playgoers should be assisted by
the events depicted in the play happening in one place
and occupying, so far as possible, no more time than
that required for their performance on the stage. *The
Alchemist*, which Coleridge classed with Sophocles'
Oedipus Tyrannus and Fielding's *Tom Jones* as 'the three
most perfect plots ever planned,' comes as near as possible
to this ideal of 'unity.'

The observance of these 'unities' of time and place
appealed to Jonson's realism; and he was essentially a
realist, even to the extent of introducing into his play
the very plague that was raging in London while he
wrote. Jonson represents the comedy of social satire at

its height. Though he made excursions into tragedy, masque and pastoral drama, his proper sphere was the satiric and comic presentation of Elizabethan and Jacobean England. In their realism his comedies differ from the romantic comedies of Shakespeare, for Jonson had none of Shakespeare's appreciation of beauty or romance. In his piercing scrutiny of human foibles and weaknesses he had no eye for subtlety of character; his men have not the complexity, nor his women the beauty, of character which Shakespeare's have; and his work, therefore, has not Shakespeare's universality. But in *The Alchemist* we see Jonson's qualities at their best. In the profession of alchemy he had a subject which appealed to his two sides: the scholar with a love of the abstruse, the satirist with an eye for the weaknesses of human nature.

THE
ALCHEMIST

Dramatis Personæ

SUBTLE, the ALCHEMIST.
FACE, the *House-keeper.*
DOL COMMON, their colleague.
DAPPER, a *Lawyer's Clerk.*
DRUGGER, a *Tobacco-man.*
LOVEWIT, *Master of the House.*
SIR EPICURE MAMMON, a *Knight.*
PERTINAX SURLY, a *Gamester.*
TRIBULATION WHOLESOME, a *Pastor* of Amsterdam.
ANANIAS, a *Deacon* there.
KASTRIL, the *angry boy.*
DAME PLIANT, his *sister,* a *Widow.*
Neighbours.

Officers, Attendants, &c.

THE SCENE
London

ACT THE FIRST

Scene I: A Room in Lovewit's House.

Enter FACE, *in a captain's uniform, with his sword drawn, and* SUBTLE *with a vial, quarrelling; and followed by* DOL COMMON.

Face. Believe 't, I will.

Sub. Thy worst. I fart at thee.

Dol. Have you your wits? why, gentlemen! for love——

Face. Sirrah, I'll strip you...out of all your sleights. *cunning*

Dol. Nay, look ye, sovereign, general, are you mad-men? *tricks*

Sub. O, let the wild sheep loose. I'll gum your silks *to be drawn*
With good strong water, an you come. *some chemical he*
is carrying

Dol. Will you have
The neighbours hear you? will you betray all?
Hark! I hear somebody.

Face. Sirrah——

Sub. I shall mar
All that the tailor has made, if you approach.

Face. You most notorious whelp, you insolent slave,
Dare you do this?

Sub. Yes, faith; yes, faith.

Face. Why, who
Am I, my mungrel? who am I?

Sub. I'll tell you,
Since you know not yourself.

Face. Speak lower, rogue.

Sub. Yes, you were once (time's not long past) the good,
Honest, plain, livery-three-pound-thrum, that kept *poorly dressed*
Your master's worship's house here in the Friers, *Blackfriars*
For the vacations——

I-2

Face. Will you be so loud?

Sub. Since, by my means, translated suburb-captain.

Face. By your means, doctor dog!

Sub. Within man's memory,

5 All this I speak of.

Face. Why, I pray you, have I

Been countenanced by you, or you by me?

Do but collect, sir, where I met you first.

Sub. I do not hear well.

10 *Face.* <u>Not of this,</u> I think it. *pun - "hear well" = good report*

But I shall put you in mind, sir;—at <u>Pie-corner,</u> *in Smithfield*

Taking your meal of steam in, from cooks' stalls,

Where, like the father of hunger, you did walk

Piteously <u>costive,</u> with your pinch'd-horn-nose, *constipated*

15 And your complexion of the Roman wash, *swarthy hue*

Stuck full of black and melancholic worms,

Like powder-corns shot at the artillery-yard.

Sub. I wish you could advance your voice a little.

Face. When you went pinn'd up in the several rags

20 You had raked and pick'd from dunghills, before day;

Your feet in mouldy slippers, for your <u>kibes;</u> *blisters*

A <u>felt</u> of rug, and a thin threaden cloak, *hat*

That scarce would cover your no buttocks—

Sub. So, sir!

25 *Face.* When all your alchemy, and your algebra,

Your minerals, vegetals, and animals,

Your conjuring, <u>cozening,</u> and your dozen of trades, *cheating*

Could not relieve your corps with so much linen

Would make you tinder, but to see a fire;

30 I gave you countenance, credit for your coals,

Your stills, your glasses, your materials;

Built you a furnace, drew you customers,

Advanced all your black arts; lent you, beside,

A house to practise in—

35 *Sub.* Your master's house!

Face. Where you have studied the more thriving skill

Of bawdry since.

Sub. Yes, in your master's house.

You and the rats here kept possession.

Make it not strange. I know you were one could keep
The buttery-hatch still lock'd, and save the chippings,
Sell the dole beer to aqua-vitæ men,
The which, together with your Christmas <u>vails</u>   *tip at :-*
5 At <u>post-and-pair</u>, your letting out of counters,   *card game*
Made you a pretty stock, some twenty marks,
And gave you credit to converse with cobwebs,
Here, since your mistress' death hath broke up house.
    Face. You might talk softlier, rascal.
10   *Sub.* No, you scarab,
I'll thunder you in pieces: I will teach you
How to beware to tempt a Fury again,
That carries tempest in his hand and voice.
    Face. The place has made you valiant.
15   *Sub.* No, your clothes.—
Thou vermin, have I ta'en thee out of dung,
So poor, so wretched, when no living thing
Would keep thee company, but a spider, or worse?
Rais'd thee from brooms, and dust, and watering-pots,
20 Sublimed thee, and exalted thee, and fix'd thee
In the third region, call'd our state of grace?
Wrought thee to spirit, to quintessence, with pains
Would twice have won me t<u>he philosopher's work?</u> *i.e. alchemy*
Put thee in words and fashion, made thee fit
25 For more than ordinary fellowships?
Giv'n thee thy oaths, thy quarrelling dimensions,
Thy rules to cheat at horse-race, cock-pit, cards,
Dice, or whatever gallant tincture else?
Made thee a second in mine own great art?
30 And have I this for thanks! Do you rebel,
Do you fly out in the <u>projection?</u> *act of throwing stone into crucible*
Would you be gone now?
    Dol. Gentlemen, what mean you?
Will you mar all?
35   *Sub.* Slave, thou hadst had no name—
    Dol. Will you undo yourselves with civil war?
    Sub. Never been known, past *equi* <u>clibanum,</u> *oven, furnace*
The heat of horse-dung, under ground, in cellars,
Or an ale-house darker than deaf John's; been lost

To all mankind, but laundresses and tapsters,
Had not I been.
    Dol. Do you know who hears you, sovereign?
    Face. Sirrah—
    Dol. Nay, general, I thought you were civil.
    Face. I shall turn desperate, if you grow thus loud.
    Sub. And hang thyself, I care not.
    Face. Hang thee, collier,
And all thy pots, and pans, in picture, I will,
Since thou hast moved me—
    Dol. O, this will o'erthrow all.
    Face. Write thee up bawd in Paul's, have all thy tricks *st.*
Of cozening with a hollow cole, dust, scrapings, *alchemists*
Searching for things lost, with a sieve and sheers, *trick*
Erecting figures in your rows of houses, *in astrology*
And taking in of shadows with a glass, *crystal*
Told in red letters; and a face cut for thee,
Worse than Gamaliel Ratsey's. *highwayman - hung 1605*
    Dol. Are you sound?
Have you your senses, masters?
    Face. I will have
A book, but barely reckoning thy impostures,
Shall prove a true philosopher's stone to printers.
    Sub. Away, you trencher-rascal!
    Face. Out, you dog-leach!
The vomit of all prisons—
    Dol. Will you be
Your own destructions, gentlemen?
    Face. Still spew'd out
For lying too heavy on the basket. *eating more than fair*
                               share - jail term
    Sub. Cheater!
    Face. Bawd!
    Sub. Cow-herd!
    Face. Conjurer!
    Sub. Cut-purse!
    Face. Witch!
    Dol. O me!
We are ruin'd, lost! have you no more regard
To your reputations? where's your judgment? 'slight,

Have yet some care of me, of your republic—
  Face. Away, this brach! I'll bring thee, rogue,
    within
The statute of sorcery, tricesimo tertio
Of Harry the eighth: ay, and perhaps, thy neck
Within a noose, for <u>laundring gold</u> and <u>barbing</u> it. *washing in acid*
  Dol. [*Snatches* FACE'S *sword.*] You'll bring your head *paring*
    within a cockscomb, will you?
And you, sir, with your <u>menstrue</u>—[*dashes* SUBTLE'S *vial* *solvent*
    out of his hand.]—gather it up.—
'Sdeath, you abominable pair of stinkards,
Leave off your barking, and grow one again,
Or, by the light that shines, I'll cut your throats.
I'll not be made a prey unto the marshal,
For ne'er a snarling <u>dog-bolt</u> of you both. *contemptible fellow*
Have you together cozen'd all this while,
And all the world, and shall it now be said,
You've made most courteous shift to cozen yourselves?
You will accuse him! you will *bring him in*   [*to* FACE.
Within the statute! Who shall take your word?
A whoreson, upstart, apocryphal captain,
Whom not a Puritan in Blackfriers will trust
So much as for a feather: and you, too,   [*to* SUBTLE.
Will give the cause, forsooth! you will insult,
And claim a primacy in the divisions!
You must be chief! as if you only had
The powder to project with, and the work
Were not begun out of equality?
The venture tripartite? all things in common?
Without priority? 'Sdeath! you perpetual curs,
Fall to your couples again, and cozen kindly,
And heartily, and lovingly, as you should,
And lose not the beginning of a <u>term,</u> *i.e. term of court.*
Or, by this hand, I shall grow factious too,
And take my part, and quit you.
  Face. 'Tis his fault;
He ever murmurs, and objects his pains,
And says, the weight of all lies upon him.
  Sub. Why, so it does.

Dol. How does it? do not we
Sustain our parts?

Sub. Yes, but they are not equal.

Dol. Why, if your part exceed to-day, I hope
Ours may, to-morrow, match it.

Sub. Ay, they *may.*

Dol. May, murmuring mastiff! ay, and do. Death on
   me!
Help me to throttle him. [*Seizes* SUB. *by the throat.*

Sub. Dorothy! mistress Dorothy!
'Ods precious, I'll do any thing. What do you mean?

Dol. Because o' your <u>fermentation and cibation</u>? *processes in alchemy*

Sub. Not I, by heaven——

Dol. Your <u>Sol and Luna</u>—help me.   [*to* FACE. *gold silver*

Sub. Would I were hang'd then! I'll conform myself.

Dol. Will you, sir? do so then, and quickly: swear.

Sub. What should I swear?

Dol. To leave your faction, sir,
And labour kindly in the common work.

Sub. Let me not breathe if I meant aught beside.
I only used those speeches as a spur
To him.

Dol. I hope we need no spurs, sir. Do we?

Face. 'Slid, prove to-day, who shall shark best.

Sub. Agreed.

Dol. Yes, and work close and friendly.

Sub. 'Slight, the knot
Shall grow the stronger for this breach, with me.
                     [*They shake hands.*

Dol. Why, so, my good baboons! Shall we go make
A sort of sober, scurvy, precise neighbours,
That scarce have smiled twice since the king came in,
A feast of laughter at our follies? Rascals,
Would run themselves from breath, to see me ride, *a punishment*
Or you t' have but a hole to thrust your heads in,
For which you should pay <u>ear-rent</u>? No, agree. *lose your ears in pillory*
And may <u>don Provost</u> ride a feasting long, *commissioner of Police*
In his old velvet jerkin and stain'd scarfs,
My noble sovereign, and worthy general,

Ere we contribute a new <u>crewel</u> garter   *yarn*
To his most worsted worship.
  Sub. Royal Dol!
Spoken like Claridiana, and thyself.
  Face. For which at supper, thou shalt sit in triumph,
And not be styled Dol Common, but Dol Proper...
                     [*Bell rings without.*
  Sub. Who's that? one rings. To the window, Dol:
   [*Exit* DOL.]—pray heaven,
The master do not trouble us this quarter.
  Face. O, fear not him. While there dies one a week
O' the plague, he's safe, from thinking toward London:
Beside, he's busy at his hop-yards now;
I had a letter from him. If he do,
He'll send such word, for airing of the house,
As you shall have sufficient time to quit it:
Though we break up a fortnight, 'tis no matter.

Re-enter DOL.

  Sub. Who is it, Dol?
  Dol. A fine young <u>quodling</u>. *a 'green' youth*
  Face. O,
My lawyer's clerk, I lighted on last night,
In Holborn, at the <u>Dagger.</u> He would have *gambling house*
(I told you of him) a <u>familiar,</u> *an attendant spirit,*
To <u>rifle</u> with at horses, and win cups. *raffle, play at dice.*
  Dol. O, let him in.
  Sub. Stay. Who shall do't?
  Face. Get you
Your robes on: I will meet him, as going out.
  Dol. And what shall I do?
  Face. Not be seen; away!   [*Exit* DOL.
Seem you very reserv'd.
  Sub. Enough.   [*Exit.*
  Face. [*aloud and retiring.*] God be wi' you, sir,
I pray you let him know that I was here:
His name is Dapper. I would gladly have staid, but——
  Dap. [*within.*] Captain, I am here.
  Face. Who's that?—He's come, I think, doctor.

Enter DAPPER.

Good faith, sir, I was going away.

   Dap. In truth,

I am very sorry, captain.

   Face. But I thought

Sure I should meet you.

   Dap. Ay, I am very glad.

I had a scurvy writ or two to make,

And I had lent my watch last night to one

That dines to-day at the sheriff's, and so was robb'd

Of my pass-time.

Re-enter SUBTLE *in his velvet cap and gown.*

Is this the cunning-man?

   Face. This is his worship.

   Dap. Is he a doctor?

   Face. Yes.

   Dap. And have you broke with him, captain?

   Face. Ay.

   Dap. And how?

   Face. Faith, he does make the matter, sir, so dainty,

I know not what to say.

   Dap. Not so, good captain.

   Face. Would I were fairly rid of it, believe me.

   Dap. Nay, now you grieve me, sir. Why should you
     wish so?

I dare assure you, I'll not be ungrateful.

   Face. I cannot think you will, sir. But the law

Is such a thing—and then he says, <u>Read</u>'s matter *Prof. of Phys.*

Falling so lately. *charged with*

   Dap. Read! he was an ass, *astrology 16?*

And dealt, sir, with a fool.

   Face. It was a clerk, sir.

   Dap. A clerk!

   Face. Nay, hear me, sir, you know the law

Better, I think—

   Dap. I should, sir, and the danger:

You know, I shew'd the statute to you.

Face. You did so.

Dap. And will I tell then! By this hand of flesh,
Wou.d it might never write good <u>court-hand</u> more, *writing style at court.*
If I discover. What do you think of me,
That I am a <u>chiaus</u>? *Turkish messenger-envoy; also swindler*
    Face. What's that?
    Dap. The Turk was here.
As one would say, do you think I am a Turk?
    Face. I'll tell the doctor so.
    Dap. Do, good sweet captain.
    Face. Come, noble doctor, pray thee let's prevail;
This is the gentleman, and he is no <u>chiaus</u>.
    Sub. Captain, I have return'd you all my answer.
I would do much, sir, for your love——But this
I neither may, nor can.
    Face. Tut, do not say so.
You deal now with a noble fellow, doctor,
One that will thank you richly; and he is no chiaus:
Let that, sir, move you.
    Sub. Pray you, forbear——
    Face. He has
Four angels here.
    Sub. You do me wrong, good sir.
    Face. Doctor, wherein? to tempt you with these
      spirits?
    Sub. To tempt my art and love, sir, to my peril.
Fore heaven, I scarce can think you are my friend,
That so would draw me to apparent danger.
    Face. I draw you! <u>a horse draw you</u>, and a halter, *i.e. to gallows*
You, and your flies together—— *attendant demons*
    Dap. Nay, good captain.
    Face. That know no difference of men.
    Sub. Good words, sir.
    Face. Good deeds, sir, doctor dogs-meat. 'Slight,
      I bring you
No cheating <u>Clim o' the Cloughs, or Claribels</u>, *heros of old ballads*
That look as big as <u>five-and-fifty, and flush;</u> *card-term - Primero*
And spit out secrets like hot custard——
    Dap. Captain!

Face. Nor any melancholic under-scribe,
Shall tell the vicar; but a special gentle,
That is the heir to forty marks a year,
Consorts with the small poets of the time,
Is the sole hope of his old grandmother;
That knows the law, and writes you six fair hands,
Is a fine clerk, and has his cyphering perfect,
Will take his oath o' the Greek Testament,
If need be, in his pocket; and can court
His mistress out of Ovid.
    Dap. Nay, dear captain——
    Face. Did you not tell me so?
    Dap. Yes; but I'd have you
Use master doctor with some more respect.
    Face. Hang him, proud stag, with his broad velvet
        head !—
But for your sake, I'd choke, ere I would change
An article of breath with such a <u>puckfist</u>: *close-fisted person*
Come, let's be gone.   [*Going.*
    Sub. Pray you let me speak with you.
    Dap. His worship calls you, captain.
    Face. I am sorry
I e'er embark'd myself in such a business.
    Dap. Nay, good sir; he did call you.
    Face. Will he take then?
    Sub. First, hear me——
    Face. Not a syllable, 'less you take.
    Sub. Pray you, sir——
    Face. Upon no terms, but an *assumpsit*.
    Sub. Your humour must be law.
                    [*He takes the four angels.*
    Face. Why now, sir, talk.
Now I dare hear you with mine honour. Speak.
So may this gentleman too.
    Sub. Why, sir——   [*Offering to whisper* FACE.
    Face. No whispering.
    Sub. Fore heaven, you do not apprehend the loss
You do your self in this.
    Face. Wherein? for what?

Sub. Marry, to be so importunate for one,
That, when he has it, will undo you all:
He'll win up all the money in the town.
    Face. How!
    Sub. Yes, and blow up gamester after gamester,
As they do crackers in a puppet-play.
If I do give him a familiar,
Give you him all you play for; never set him:
For he will have it.
    Face. You are mistaken, doctor.
Why, he does ask one but for cups and horses,
A rifling fly; none of your great familiars.
    Dap. Yes, captain, I would have it for all games.
    Sub. I told you so.
    Face. [*Taking* DAP. *aside.*] 'Slight, that is a new
      business!
I understood you, a tame <u>bird,</u> to fly   *familiar spirit*
Twice in a term, or so, on Friday nights,
When you had left the office, for a nag
Of forty or fifty shillings.
    Dap. Ay, 'tis true, sir;
But I do think now I shall leave the law,
And therefore——
    Face. Why, this changes quite the case.
Do you think that I dare move him?
    Dap. If you please, sir;
All's one to him, I see.
    Face. What! for that money?
I cannot with my conscience; nor should you
Make the request, methinks.
    Dap. No, sir, I mean
To add consideration.
    Face. Why then, sir,
I'll try.—[*Goes to* SUBTLE.] Say that it were for all games,
    doctor?
    Sub. I say then, not a mouth shall eat for him
At any ordinary, but on the score,
That is a gaming mouth, conceive me.
    Face. Indeed!

Sub. He'll draw you all the treasure of the realm,
If it be set him.

Face. Speak you this from art?

Sub. Ay, sir, and reason too, the ground of art.
He is of the only best complexion,
The queen of Fairy loves.

Face. What! is he?

Sub. Peace.
He'll overhear you. Sir, should she but see him——

Face. What?

Sub. Do not you tell him.

Face. Will he win at cards too?

Sub. The spirits of <u>dead Holland, living Isaac,</u> *gamblero*
You'd swear, were in him; such a vigorous luck
As cannot be resisted. 'Slight, he'll put
<u>Six of your gallants to a cloak</u>, indeed. *to win all, except dead*

Face. A strange success, that some man shall be born
  to!

Sub. He hears you, man——

Dap. Sir, I'll not be ingrateful.

Face. Faith, I have confidence in his good nature:
You hear, he says he will not be ingrateful.

Sub. Why, as you please; my venture follows yours.

Face. Troth, do it, doctor; think him trusty, and
  make him.
He may make us both happy in an hour;
Win some five thousand pound, and send us two on't.

Dap. Believe it, and I will, sir.

Face. And you shall, sir.   [*Takes him aside.*
You have heard all?

Dap. No, what was't? Nothing, I, sir.

Face. Nothing!

Dap. A little, sir.

Face. Well, a rare star
Reign'd at your birth.

Dap. At mine, sir! No.

Face The doctor
Swears that you are——

Sub. Nay, captain, you'll tell all now.

Face. Allied to the queen of Fairy.
    Dap. Who? that I am?
Believe it, no such matter—
    Face. Yes, and that
You were born with a <u>cawl</u> on your head. *membrane*
    Dap. Who says so?
    Face. Come,
You know it well enough, though you dissemble it.
    Dap. I'fac, I do not: you are mistaken. *I'faith*
    Face. How!
Swear by your fac, and in a thing so known
Unto the doctor? how shall we, sir, trust you
In the other matter? can we ever think,
When you have won five or six thousand pound,
You'll send us shares in't, by this rate?
    Dap. By Jove, sir,
I'll win ten thousand pound, and send you half.
I' fac's no oath.
    Sub. No, no, he did but jest.
    Face. Go to. Go thank the doctor: he's your friend,
To take it so.
    Dap. I thank his worship.
    Face. So!
Another angel.
    Dap. Must I?
    Face. Must you! 'slight,
What else is thanks? will you be trivial?—Doctor,
                    [DAPPER *gives him the money*
When must he come for his familiar?
    Dap. Shall I not have it with me?
    Sub. O, good sir!
There must a world of ceremonies pass;
You must be bath'd and fumigated first:
Besides, the queen of Fairy does not rise
Till it be noon.
    Face. Not, if she danced, to-night.
    Sub. And she must bless it.
    Face. Did you never see
Her royal grace yet?

Dap. Whom?

Face. Your aunt of Fairy?

Sub. Not since she kist him in the cradle, captain;
I can resolve you that.

Face. Well, see her grace,
Whate'er it cost you, for a thing that I know.
It will be somewhat hard to compass; but
However, see her. You are made, believe it,
If you can see her. Her grace is a lone woman,
And very rich; and if she take a fancy,
She will do strange things. See her, at any hand.
'Slid, she may hap to leave you all she has:
It is the doctor's fear.

Dap. How will't be done, then?

Face. Let me alone, take you no thought. Do you
But say to me, captain, I'll see her grace.

Dap. *Captain, I'll see her grace.*

Face. Enough.   [*Knocking within.*

Sub. Who's there?
Anon.—Conduct him forth by the back way.—
                                   [*Aside to* FACE.
Sir, against one o'clock prepare yourself;
Till when you must be fasting; only take
Three drops of vinegar in at your nose,
Two at your mouth, and one at either ear;
Then bathe your fingers' ends and wash your eyes,
To sharpen your five senses, and cry *hum*
Thrice, and then *buz* as often; and then come.   [*Exit.*

Face. Can you remember this?

Dap. I warrant you.

Face. Well then, away. It is but your bestowing
Some twenty nobles 'mong her grace's servants,
And put on a clean shirt: you do not know
What grace her grace may do you in clean linen.
                     [*Exeunt* FACE *and* DAPPER.

Sub. [*within.*] Come in! Good wives, I pray you
    forbear me now;
Troth I can do you no good till afternoon—

Re-enters, followed by DRUGGER.

What is your name, say you, Abel Drugger?
　Drug. Yes, sir.
　Sub. A seller of tobacco?
　Drug. Yes, sir.
　Sub. Umph!
Free of the grocers?　*member of Grocers' Company*
　Drug. Ay, an't please you.
　Sub. Well——
Your business, Abel?
　Drug. This, an't please your worship;
I am a young beginner, and am building
Of a new shop, an't like your worship, just
At corner of a street:—Here is the plot on't—
And I would know by art, sir, of your worship,
Which way I should make my door, by necromancy,
And where my shelves; and which should be for boxes,
And which for pots. I would be glad to thrive, sir:
And I was wish'd to your worship by a gentleman,
One captain Face, that says you know men's planets,
And their good <u>angels</u>, and their bad.　*also means 'a coin' here*
　Sub. I do,
If I do see them——　*play on 2 meanings of "angels"*

Re-enter FACE.

　Face. What! my honest Abel?
Thou art well met here.
　Drug. Troth, sir, I was speaking,
Just as your worship came here, of your worship:
I pray you speak for me to master doctor.
　Face. He shall do any thing.—Doctor, do you hear?
This is my friend, Abel, an honest fellow;
He lets me have good tobacco, and he does not
<u>Sophisticate</u> it with sack-lees or oil,　*adulterate*
Nor washes it in muscadel and <u>grains</u>,　*spices*
Nor buries it in gravel, under ground,...
But keeps it in fine lily pots, that, open'd,
Smell like conserve of roses, or French beans.

He has his <u>maple block, his silver tongs</u>, *conveniences in*
Winchester pipes, and fire of juniper: *thereconists*
A neat, spruce, honest fellow, and no goldsmith.—*also moneyle*

   Sub. He is a fortunate fellow, that I am sure on.
   Face. Already, sir, have you found it? Lo thee, Abel!
   Sub. And in right way toward riches—
   Face. Sir!
   Sub. This summer
He will be of the <u>clothing of his company,</u> *i.e. liveryman of C*
And next spring <u>call'd to the scarlet</u>; spend what he can. *mad*
                                                 sherif
   Face. What, and so little beard?
   Sub. Sir, you must think,
He may have a receipt to make hair come:
But he'll be wise, preserve his youth, and <u>fine for't</u>; *i.e. for*
His fortune looks for him another way. *refusing o*
   Face. 'Slid, doctor, how canst thou know this so soon?
I am <u>amused</u> at that! *amazed*
   Sub. By a rule, captain,
In <u>metoposcopy</u>, which I do work by; *reading character from*
A certain star in the forehead, which you see not.
Your chestnut or your olive-colour'd face
Does never fail: and your long ear doth promise.
I knew't, by certain spots, too, in his teeth,
And on the nail of his mercurial finger.
   Face. Which finger's that?
   Sub. His little finger. Look.
You were born upon a Wednesday?
   Drug. Yes, indeed, sir.
   Sub. The thumb, in chiromancy, we give Venus;
The fore-finger, to Jove; the midst, to Saturn;
The ring, to Sol; the least, to Mercury,
Who was the lord, sir, of his horoscope,
His house of life being Libra; which fore-shew'd,
He should be a merchant, and should trade with balance.
   Face. Why, this is strange! Is it not, honest Nab?
   Sub. There is a ship now, coming from <u>Ormus</u>, *on Persian*
That shall yield him such a commodity *Gulf*
Of drugs—This is the west, and this the south?
                                 [Pointing to the plan.

Drug. Yes, sir.

Sub. And those are your two sides?

Drug. Ay, sir.

Sub. Make me your door, then, south; your broad side, west:
And on the east side of your shop, aloft,
Write Mathlai, Tarmiel, and Baraborat;
Upon the north part, Rael, Velel, Thiel.
They are the names of those Mercurial spirits,
That do fright flies from boxes.

Drug. Yes, sir.

Sub. And
Beneath your threshold, bury me a load-stone
To draw in gallants that wear spurs: the rest,
They'll <u>seem to</u> follow. *deem it seemly to*

Face. That's a secret, Nab!

Sub. And, on your stall, a puppet, with a vice *machinery for*
And a court-<u>fucus</u>, to call city-dames: *cosmetics / moving wires*
You shall deal much with minerals.

Drug. Sir, I have
At home, already——

Sub. Ay, I know you have arsenic,
Vitriol, sal-tartar, argaile, alkali,
Cinoper: I know all.—This fellow, captain,
Will come, in time, to be a great distiller,
And give a say—I will not say directly,
But very fair—at the philosopher's stone.

Face. Why, how now, Abel! is this true?

Drug. Good captain,
What must I give?   [*Aside to* FACE.

Face. Nay, I'll not counsel thee.
Thou hear'st what wealth (he says, spend what thou canst,)
Thou'rt like to come to.

Drug I would gi' him a crown.

Face. A crown! and toward such a fortune? heart,
Thou shalt rather gi' him thy shop. No gold about thee?

Drug. Yes, I have a <u>portague,</u> I have kept this half *gold coin*
year.

Face. Out on thee, Nab! 'Slight, there was such an
  offer—
Shalt keep't no longer, I'll give't him for thee.—Doctor,
Nab prays your worship to drink this, and swears
He will appear more grateful, as your skill
Does raise him in the world.
    Drug. I would entreat
Another favour of his worship.
    Face. What is't, Nab?
    Drug. But to look over, sir, my almanack,
And cross out my ill-days, that I may neither
Bargain, nor trust upon them.
    Face. That he shall, Nab:
Leave it, it shall be done, 'gainst afternoon.
    Sub. And a direction for his shelves.
    Face. Now, Nab,
Art thou well pleased, Nab?
    Drug. 'Thank, sir, both your worships.
    Face. Away.—   [*Exit* DRUGGER.
Why, now, you smoaky persecutor of nature!
Now do you see, that something's to be done,
Beside your beech-coal, and your corsive waters,
Your crosslets, crucibles, and cucurbites?
You must have stuff, brought home to you, to work on:
And yet you think, I am at no expense
In searching out these veins, then following them,
Then trying them out. 'Fore God, my intelligence
Costs me more money, than my share oft comes to,
In these rare works.
    Sub. You are pleasant, sir.—

          Re-enter DOL.

          How now!
What says my dainty Dolkin?
    Dol. Yonder fish-wife
Will not away. And there's your giantess,
The bawd of Lambeth.
    Sub. Heart, I cannot speak with them.
    Dol. Not afore night, I have told them in a voice,

Thorough the <u>trunk,</u> like one of your familiars. *speaking tube*
But I have spied sir Epicure Mammon——
   Sub. Where?
   Dol. Coming along, at far end of the lane,
Slow of his feet, but earnest of his tongue
To one that's with him.
   Sub. Face, go you, and shift.   [*Exit* FACE
Dol, you must presently make ready, too.
   Dol. Why, what's the matter?
   Sub. O, I did look for him
With the sun's rising: 'marvel he could sleep.
This is the day I am to perfect for him
The magisterium, our great work, the stone;
And yield it, made, into his hands: of which
He has, this month, talk'd as he were possess'd.
And now he's dealing pieces on't away.—
Methinks I see him entering ordinaries,
Dispensing for the pox, and plaguy houses,
<u>Reaching his dose,</u> walking Moor-fields for lepers, *offering his*
And offering citizens' wives <u>pomander-bracelets,</u> *remedy*
As his preservative, made of the elixir;... *philosopher's stone*
I see no end of his labours. He will make
Nature asham'd of her long sleep: when art,
Who's but a step-dame, shall do more then she,
In her best love to mankind, ever could:
If his dream last, he'll turn the age to gold.   [*Exeunt.*

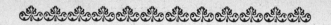

ACT THE SECOND

SCENE I: An outer Room in LOVEWIT'S House.

Enter Sir EPICURE MAMMON *and* SURLY.

Mam. Come on, sir. Now, you set your foot on shore
In *Novo Orbe*; here's the rich Peru:
And there within, sir, are the golden mines,
Great Solomon's Ophir! he was sailing to't,
Three years, but we have reach'd it in ten months.
This is the day, wherein, to all my friends,
I will pronounce the happy word, BE RICH;
THIS DAY YOU SHALL BE SPECTATISSIMI.
You shall no more deal with the hollow dye, *loaded dice*
Or the frail card. No more be at charge of keeping
The livery-punk for the young heir, that must
Seal, at all hours, in his shirt: no more,
If he deny, have him beaten to't, as he is
That brings him the commodity. No more
Shall thirst of satin, or the covetous hunger
Of velvet entrails for a rude-spun cloke, *lining*
To be display'd at madam Augusta's, make *gambling den*
The sons of Sword and Hazard fall before *gamblers*
The golden calf, and on their knees, whole nights,
Commit idolatry with wine and trumpets:
Or go a feasting after drum and ensign....
And unto thee I speak it first, BE RICH.
Where is my Subtle, there? Within, ho!
  Face. [*within.*] Sir, he'll come to you by and by.
  Mam. That is his fire-drake, *alchemist's assistant*
His Lungs, his Zephyrus, he that puffs his coals, *looked after*
Till he firk nature up, in her own centre. *arouse*
You are not faithful, sir. This night, I'll change *believing*
All that is metal, in my house, to gold:
And, early in the morning, will I send
To all the plumbers and the pewterers,

And buy their tin and lead up; and to <u>Lothbury</u>   street where
                                                        founders live
For all the copper.

   Sur. What, and turn that too?

   Mam. Yes, and I'll purchase Devonshire, and Corn-
     wall,

<u>And make them perfect Indies</u>! you admire now?   Change their
                                                       tin to gold

   Sur. No, faith.

   Mam. But when you see th' effects of the Great
     Medicine,

Of which one part projected on a hundred

Of Mercury, or <u>Venus</u>, or the <u>moon</u>,   Copper ~ gold
                                                  silver
Shall turn it to as many of the <u>sun</u>;

Nay, to a thousand, so ad infinitum:

You will believe me.

   Sur. Yes, when I see't, I will....

   Mam. Do you think I fable with you? I assure you,

He that has once the flower of the sun,

The perfect ruby, which we call elixir,

Not only can do that, but, by its virtue,

Can confer honour, love, respect, long life;

Give safety, valour, yea, and victory,

To whom he will. In eight and twenty days,

I'll make an old man of fourscore, a child.

   Sur. No doubt; he's that already.

   Mam. Nay, I mean,

Restore his years, renew him, like an eagle,

To the fifth age; make him get sons and daughters,

Young giants; as our philosophers have done,

The ancient patriarchs, afore the flood,

But taking, once a week, on a knife's point,

The quantity of a grain of mustard of it;

Become stout Marses, and beget young Cupids.

   ...'Tis the secret

Of nature naturized 'gainst all infections,

Cures all diseases coming of all causes;

A month's grief in a day, a year's in twelve;

And, of what age soever, in a month:

Past all the doses of your drugging doctors.

I'll undertake, withall, to fright the plague

Out of the kingdom in three months.
    Sur. And I'll
Be bound, the players shall sing your praises, then,
Without their poets.
    Mam. Sir, I'll do't. Meantime,
I'll give away so much unto my man,
Shall serve the whole city, with preservative,
Weekly; each house his dose, and at the rate——

Bevis Bulmer

    Sur. As <u>he that built the Water-work</u>, does with
      water?
    Mam. You are incredulous.
    Sur. Faith I have a humour,
I would not willingly be gull'd. Your stone
Cannot transmute me.
    Mam. Pertinax, [my] Surly,
Will you believe antiquity? records?
I'll shew you a book where Moses and his sister,
And Solomon have written of the art;
Ay, and a treatise penn'd by Adam——
    Sur. How!
    Mam. Of the philosopher's stone, and in High Dutch.
    Sur. Did Adam write, sir, in High Dutch?
    Mam. He did;
Which proves it was the primitive tongue.
    Sur. What paper?
    Mam. On cedar board.
    Sur. O that, indeed, they say,
Will last 'gainst worms.
    Mam. 'Tis like your Irish wood,
'Gainst cob-webs. I have a piece of <u>Jason's fleece</u>, too,

association of mythology & alchemy

Which was no other than a book of alchemy,
Writ in large sheep-skin, a good fat ram-vellum.
Such was Pythagoras' thigh, Pandora's tub,
And, all that fable of Medea's charms,
The manner of our work; the bulls, our furnace,
Still breathing fire; our argent-vive, the dragon: *mercury*
The dragon's teeth, mercury sublimate,
That keeps the whiteness, hardness, and the biting;
And they are gather'd into Jason's helm,

The alembic, and then sow'd in Mars his field, *cap of distilling apparatus*
And thence sublimed so often, till they're fix'd.
Both this, the Hesperian garden, Cadmus' story,
Jove's shower, the boon of Midas, Argus' eyes, *allusion to Danaë*
Boccace his Demogorgon, thousands more, *a demon*
All abstract riddles of our stone.—

Enter FACE, *as a servant.*

                        How now!
Do we succeed? Is our day come? and holds it?
  Face. The evening will set red upon you, sir;
You have colour for it, crimson: the red ferment
Has done his office; three hours hence prepare you
To see projection.
  Mam. Pertinax, my Surly,
Again I say to thee, aloud, Be rich.
This day, thou shalt have ingots; and, to-morrow,
Give lords th' affront.—Is it, my Zephyrus, right?
Blushes the bolt's-head? *glass vessel with long neck.*
  Face. Like a wench with child, sir,
That were but now discover'd to her master.
  Mam. Excellent witty Lungs!—my only care is,
Where to get stuff enough now, to project on;
This town will not half serve me.
  Face. No, sir! buy
The covering off o' churches.
  Mam. That's true.
  Face. Yes.
Let them stand bare, as do their auditory;
Or cap them, new, with shingles. *wooden house tiles*
  Mam. No, good thatch:
Thatch will lie light upon the rafters, Lungs.—
Lungs, I will manumit thee from the furnace,
I will restore thee thy complexion, Puffe,
Lost in the embers; and repair this brain,
Hurt with the fume o' the metals.
  Face. I have blown, sir,
Hard for your worship; thrown by many a coal,
When 'twas not beech; weigh'd those I put in, just,

To keep your heat still even; these blear'd eyes
Have wak'd to read your several colours, sir,   *i.e. assumed*
Of the pale citron, the green lion, the crow,   *by processes of*
The peacock's tail, the plumed swan.   *alchemy*
   Mam. And, lastly,
Thou hast descried the flower, the *sanguis agni*?
   Face. Yes, sir.
   Mam. Where's master?
   Face. At his prayers, sir, he;
Good man, he's doing his devotions
For the success.
   Mam. Lungs, I will set a period
To all thy labours; thou shalt be the master
Of my seraglio.   *harem*
   Face. Good, sir.
   Mam. But do you hear?...
Thou art sure thou saw'st it blood?
   Face. Both blood and spirit, sir.
   Mam. I will have all my beds blown up, not stuft:
Down is too hard: and then, mine oval room
Fill'd with such pictures as Tiberius took
From Elephantis, and dull Aretine   *licentious Greek poet ×*
But coldly imitated....My flatterers   *" Italian satirist*
Shall be the pure and gravest of divines,
That I can get for money. My mere fools,
Eloquent burgesses, and then my poets
The same that writ so subtly of the fart,
Whom I will entertain still for that subject....
We will be brave, Puffe, now we have the med'cine.
My meat shall all come in, in Indian shells,
Dishes of agat set in gold, and studded
With emeralds, sapphires, hyacinths, and rubies.
The tongues of carps, dormice, and camels' heels,
Boil'd in the spirit of sol, and dissolv'd pearl,
Apicius' diet, 'gainst the epilepsy: *Roman glutton*
And I will eat these broths with spoons of amber,
Headed with diamond and carbuncle.
My foot-boy shall eat pheasants, calver'd salmons,   *cooked in*
birds of Knots, godwits, lampreys: I myself will have   *a certain*
the snipe family

The beards of <u>barbels</u> served, instead of sallads;   *mullets*
Oil'd mushrooms; and the swelling unctuous paps
Of a fat pregnant sow, newly cut off,
Drest with an exquisite, and poignant sauce;
For which, I'll say unto my cook, *There's gold,*
Go forth, and be a knight.
      Face. Sir, I'll go look
A little, how it heightens.   [*Exit.*
      Mam.—My shirts
I'll have of taffeta-sarsnet, soft and light
As cobwebs; and for all my other raiment,
It shall be such as might provoke the Persian,
Were he to teach the world riot anew.
My gloves of fishes and birds' skins, perfumed
With gums of paradise, and eastern air——
      Sur. And do you think to have the stone with this?
      Mam. No, I do think t' have all this with the stone.
      Sur. Why, I have heard, he must be *homo frugi*,
A pious, holy, and religious man,
One free from mortal sin, a very virgin.
      Mam. That makes it, sir; he is so: but I buy it;
My venture brings it me. He, honest wretch,
A notable, superstitious, good soul,
Has worn his knees bare, and his slippers bald,
With prayer and fasting for it: and, sir, let him
Do it alone, for me, still. Here he comes.
Not a profane word afore him: 'tis poison.—

                    Enter SUBTLE.

Good morrow, father.
      Sub. Gentle son, good morrow,
And to your friend there. What is he, is with you?
      Mam. An heretic, that I did bring along,
In hope, sir, to convert him.
      Sub. Son, I doubt
You are covetous, that thus you meet your time
In the just point: <u>prevent</u> your day at morning.   *anticipate*
This argues something, worthy of a fear
Of importune and carnal appetite.

Take heed you do not cause the blessing leave you,
With your ungovern'd haste. I should be sorry
To see my labours, now even at perfection,
Got by long watching and large patience,
Not prosper where my love and zeal hath placed them.
Which (heaven I call to witness, with your self,
To whom I have pour'd my thoughts) in all my ends,
Have look'd no way, but unto public good,
To pious uses, and dear charity
Now grown a prodigy with men. Wherein
If you, my son, should now prevaricate,
And, to your own particular lusts employ
So great and catholic a bliss, be sure
A curse will follow, yea, and overtake
Your subtle and most secret ways.
 Mam. I know, sir;
You shall not need to fear me: I but come,
To have you confute this gentleman.
 Sur. Who is,
Indeed, sir, somewhat costive of belief
Toward your stone; would not be gull'd.
 Sub. Well, son,
All that I can convince him in, is this,
The WORK IS DONE, bright sol is in his robe.
We have a medicine of the triple soul,
The glorified spirit. Thanks be to heaven,
And make us worthy of it!—Ulen Spiegel!
 Face. [*within.*] Anon, sir.
 Sub. Look well to the register.
And let your heat still lessen by degrees,
To the aludels.
 Face. [*within.*] Yes, sir.
 Sub. Did you look
O' the bolt's-head yet?
 Face. [*within.*] Which? on D, sir?
 Sub. Ay;
What's the complexion?
 Face. [*within.*] Whitish.
 Sub. Infuse vinegar,

To draw his volatile substance and his tincture:
And let the water in glass E be filter'd,
And put into the gripe's egg. Lute him well; *vessel shaped*
And leave him closed in balneo. *cover with mud* *like large bird's*
egg *to protect*
  Face. [*within.*] I will, sir.
  Sur. What a brave language here is! next to canting. *secret lang.*
  Sub. I have another work, you never saw, son, *of beggars*
That three days since past the philosopher's wheel,
In the lent heat of Athanor; and's become *digesting furnace*
Sulphur of Nature.
  Mam. But 'tis for me?
  Sub. What need you?
You have enough in that is perfect.
  Mam. O but——
  Sub. Why, this is covetise!
  Mam. No, I assure you,
I shall employ it all in pious uses,
Founding of colleges and grammar schools,
Marrying young virgins, building hospitals,
And now and then a church.

Re-enter FACE.

  Sub. How now!
  Face. Sir, please you,
Shall I not change the filter?
  Sub. Marry, yes;
And bring me the complexion of glass B.   [*Exit* FACE.
  Mam. Have you another?
  Sub. Yes, son; were I assured
Your piety were firm, we would not want
The means to glorify it: but I hope the best.—
I mean to tinct C in sand-heat to-morrow,
And give him imbibition. *saturation*
  Mam. Of white oil?
  Sub. No, sir, of red. F is come over the helm too, *alembic*
I thank my maker, in S. Mary's bath,
And shews *lac virginis.* Blessed be heaven! *mercury*
I sent you of his fæces there calcined:
Out of that calx, I have won the salt of mercury.

Mam. By pouring on your rectified water?
Sub. Yes, and reverberating in Athanor.

Re-enter FACE.

How now! what colour says it?
    Face. The ground black, sir.
    Mam. That's your crow's-head?
    Sur. Your cock's-comb's, is it not?
    Sub. No, 'tis not perfect. Would it were the crow!
That work wants something.
    Sur. O, I look'd for this.
The hay's a pitching.   [net for catching rabbits]   [*Aside.*
    Sub. Are you sure you loosed them
In their own menstrue?
    Face. Yes, sir, and then married them,
And put them in a bolt's-head nipp'd to digestion,   [sealed for furnace]
According as you bade me, when I set
The liquor of Mars to circulation   [iron]
In the same heat.
    Sub. The process then was right.
    Face. Yes, by the token, sir, the retort brake,
And what was saved was put into the pellican,   [glass vessel]
And sign'd with Hermes' seal.   [hermetically sealed]
    Sub. I think 'twas so.
We should have a new amalgama.
    Sur. O, this ferret
Is rank as any pole-cat.   [*Aside.*
    Sub. But I care not:
Let him e'en die; we have enough beside,
In embrion. H has his white shirt on?   [reached white stage]
    Face. Yes, sir,
He's ripe for inceration, he stands warm,   [reduction to
In his ash-fire. I would not you should let   wax-like
Any die now, if I might counsel, sir,   consistency]
For luck's sake to the rest: it is not good.
    Mam. He says right.
    Sur. Ay, are you bolted?   [*Aside.*
    Face. Nay, I know't, sir,
I have seen the ill fortune. What is some three ounces

Of fresh materials?

   Mam. Is't no more?

   Face. No more, sir,

Of gold, t'amalgame with some six of mercury.

   Mam. Away, here's money. What will serve?

   Face. Ask him, sir.

   Mam. How much?

   Sub. Give him nine pound:—you may give him ten.

   Sur. Yes, twenty, and be cozen'd, do.

   Mam. There 'tis.   [*Gives* FACE *the money.*

   Sub. This needs not; but that you will have it so,

To see conclusions of all: for two

Of our inferior works are at fixation,

A third is in ascension. Go your ways.

Have you set the oil of luna in kemia?

   Face. Yes, sir.

   Sub. And the philosopher's vinegar?

   Face. Ay.   [*Exit.*

   Sur. We shall have a sallad!

   Mam. When do you make projection?

   Sub. Son, be not hasty, I exalt our med'cine,

By hanging him *in balneo vaporoso*,

And giving him solution; then congeal him;

And then dissolve him; then again congeal him:

For look, how oft I iterate the work,

So many times I add unto his virtue.

As, if at first one ounce convert a hundred,

After his second loose, he'll turn a thousand;

His third solution, ten; his fourth, a hundred:

After his fifth, a thousand thousand ounces

Of any imperfect metal, into pure

Silver or gold, in all examinations,

As good as any of the natural mine.

Get you your stuff here against afternoon,

Your brass, your pewter, and your andirons.

   Mam. Not those of iron?

   Sub. Yes, you may bring them too:

We'll change all metals.

   Sur. I believe you in that.

    Mam. Then I may send my spits?

    Sub. Yes, and your racks.

    Sur. And dripping-pans, and pot-hangers, and hooks,
Shall he not?

    Sub. If he please.

    Sur. —To be an ass.

    Sub. How, sir!

    Mam. This gentleman you must bear withal:
I told you he had no faith.

    Sur. And little hope, sir;
But much less charity, should I gull myself.

    Sub. Why, what have you observ'd, sir, in our art,
Seems so impossible?

    Sur. But your whole work, no more.
That you should hatch gold in a furnace, sir,
As they do eggs in Egypt!

    Sub. Sir, do you
Believe that eggs are hatch'd so?

    Sur. If I should?

    Sub. Why, I think that the greater miracle.
No egg but differs from a chicken more
Than metals in themselves.

    Sur. That cannot be.
The egg's ordain'd by nature to that end,
And is a chicken *in potentia*.

    Sub. The same we say of lead and other metals,
Which would be gold, if they had time.

    Mam. And that
Our art doth further.

    Sub. Ay, for 'twere absurd
To think that nature in the earth bred gold
Perfect in the instant: something went before.
There must be remote matter.

    Sur. Ay, what is that?

    Sub. Marry, we say—

    Mam. Ay, now it heats: stand, father,
Pound him to dust.

    Sub. It is, of the one part,
A humid exhalation, which we call

Materia liquida, or the unctuous water;
On the other part, a certain crass and viscous
Portion of earth; both which, concorporate,
Do make the elementary matter of gold;
Which is not yet *propria materia*,
But common to all metals and all stones;
For, where it is forsaken of that moisture,
And hath more dryness, it becomes a stone:
Where it retains more of the humid fatness,
It turns to sulphur, or to quicksilver,
Who are the parents of all other metals.
Nor can this remote matter suddenly
Progress so from extreme unto extreme,
As to grow gold, and leap o'er all the means.
Nature doth first beget the imperfect, then
Proceeds she to the perfect. Of that airy
And oily water, mercury is engender'd;
Sulphur of the fat and earthy part; the one,
Which is the last, supplying the place of male,
The other of the female, in all metals.
Some do believe hermaphrodeity,
That both do act and suffer. But these two
Make the rest ductile, malleable, extensive.
And even in gold they are; for we do find
Seeds of them, by our fire, and gold in them;
And can produce the species of each metal
More perfect thence, than nature doth in earth.
Beside, who doth not see in daily practice
Art can beget bees, hornets, beetles, wasps,
Out of the carcasses and dung of creatures;
Yea, scorpions of an herb, being rightly placed?
And these are living creatures, far more perfect
And excellent than metals.
    Mam. Well said, father!
Nay, if he take you in hand, sir, with an argument,
He'll bray you in a mortar.
    Sur. Pray you, sir, stay.
Rather than I'll be bray'd, sir, I'll believe
That Alchemy is a pretty kind of game,

Somewhat like tricks o' the cards, to cheat a man
With charming.
  Sub. Sir?
  Sur. What else are all your terms,
Whereon no one of your writers 'grees with other?
Of your elixir, your *lac virginis*,
Your stone, your med'cine, and your chrysosperme,
Your sal, your sulphur, and your mercury,
Your oil of height, your tree of life, your blood,
Your marchesite, your tutie, your magnesia,
Your toad, your crow, your dragon, and your panther;
Your sun, your moon, your firmament, your adrop,
Your lato, azoch, zernich, chibrit, heautarit,
And then your red man, and your white woman,
With all your broths, your menstrues, and materials,...
Hair o' the head, burnt clouts, chalk, merds, and clay,
Powder of bones, scalings of iron, glass,
And worlds of other strange ingredients,
Would burst a man to name?
  Sub. And all these named,
Intending but one thing; which art our writers
Used to obscure their art.
  Mam. Sir, so I told him—
Because the simple idiot should not learn it,
And make it vulgar.
  Sub. Was not all the knowledge
Of the Ægyptians writ in mystic symbols?
Speak not the scriptures oft in parables?
Are not the choicest fables of the poets,
That were the fountains and first springs of wisdom,
Wrapp'd in perplexed allegories?
  Mam. I urg'd that,
And clear'd to him, that Sisyphus was damn'd
To roll the ceaseless stone, only because
He would have made Ours common. [DOL *appears at
    the door.*]—Who is this?
  Sub. 'S precious!—What do you mean? go in, good
    lady,
Let me entreat you. [DOL *retires.*]—Where's this varlet?

Re-enter FACE.

Face. Sir.

Sub. You very knave! do you use me thus?

Face. Wherein, sir?

Sub. Go in and see, you traitor. Go!   [*Exit* FACE.

Mam. Who is it, sir?

Sub. Nothing, sir; nothing.

Mam. What's the matter, good sir?

I have not seen you thus distemper'd: who is't?

Sub. All arts have still had, sir, their adversaries;

But ours the most ignorant.—

Re-enter FACE.

What now?

Face. 'Twas not my fault, sir; she would speak with
    you.

Sub. Would she, sir! Follow me.   [*Exit*

Mam. [*stopping him.*] Stay, Lungs.

Face. I dare not, sir.

Mam. Stay, man; what is she?

Face. A lord's sister, sir.

Mam. How! pray thee, stay.

Face. She's mad, sir, and sent hither—

He'll be mad too.—

Mam. I warrant thee.—

Why sent hither?

Face. Sir, to be cured.

Sub. [*within.*] Why, rascal!

Face. Lo you!—Here, sir!   [*Exit.*

Mam. 'Fore God, a Bradamante, a brave piece.

Sur. Heart, this is a bawdy-house! I will be burnt
    else.

Mam. O, by this light, no: do not wrong him. He's
Too scrupulous that way: it is his vice.
No, he's a rare physician, do him right,
An excellent Paracelsian, and has done
Strange cures with mineral physic. He deals all
With spirits, he; he will not hear a word
Of Galen, or his tedious recipes.—

Re-enter FACE.

How now, Lungs!

    Face. Softly, sir; speak softly. I meant
To have told your worship all. This must not hear.

    Mam. No, he will not be "gull'd:" let him alone.

    Face. You are very right, sir; she is a most rare scholar,
And is gone mad with studying Broughton's works.
If you but name a word touching the Hebrew,
She falls into her fit, and will discourse
So learnedly of genealogies,
As you would run mad too, to hear her, sir.

    Mam. How might one do t' have conference with her,
      Lungs?

    Face. O divers have run mad upon the conference
I do not know, sir. I am sent in haste,
To fetch a vial.

    Sur. Be not gull'd, sir Mammon.

    Mam. Wherein? pray ye, be patient.

    Sur. Yes, as you are,
And trust confederate knaves and bawds and whores.

    Mam. You are too foul, believe it.—Come here, Ulen,
One word.

    Face. I dare not, in good faith.   [*Going.*

    Mam. Stay, knave.

    Face. He is extreme angry that you saw her, sir.

    Mam. Drink that. [*Gives him money.*] What is she
    when she's out of her fit?

    Face. O, the most affablest creature, sir! so merry!
So pleasant!...

    Sub. [*within.*] Ulen!

    Face. I'll come to you again, sir.   [*Exit.*

    Mam. Surly, I did not think one of your breeding
Would traduce personages of worth.

    Sur. Sir Epicure,
Your friend to use; yet still, loth to be gull'd:
I do not like your philosophical bawds.
Their stone is letchery enough to pay for,
Without this bait.

Mam. 'Heart, you abuse your self.
I know the lady, and her friends, and means,
The original of this disaster. Her brother
Has told me all.

Sur. And yet you never saw her
Till now!

Mam. O yes, but I forgot. I have, believe it,
One of the treacherousest memories, I do think,
Of all mankind.

Sur. What call you her brother?

Mam. My lord—
He will not have his name known, now I think on't.

Sur. A very treacherous memory!

Mam. On my faith—

Sur. Tut, if you have it not about you, pass it,
Till we meet next.

Mam. Nay, by this hand, 'tis true.
He's one I honour, and my noble friend;
And I respect his house.

Sur. Heart! can it be,
That a grave sir, a rich, that has no need,
A wise sir, too, at other times, should thus,
With his own oaths, and arguments, make hard means
To gull himself? An this be your elixir,
Your *lapis mineralis*, and your lunary,
Give me your honest trick yet at primero,
Or gleek; and take your *lutum sapientis*,
Your *menstruum simplex!* I'll have gold before you,
And with less danger....

Re-enter FACE.

Face. Here's one from captain Face, sir, [*to* SURLY.]
Desires you meet him in the Temple-church,
Some half hour hence, and upon earnest business.
Sir, [*whispers* MAMMON.] if you please to quit us, now;
     and come
Again within two hours, you shall have
My master busy examining o' the works;
And I will steal you in, unto the party,

That you may see her converse.—Sir, shall I say,
You'll meet the captain's worship?

    Sur. Sir, I will.—   *[Walks aside.*

But, by attorney, and to a second purpose.
Now, I am sure it is a bawdy-house;
I'll swear it, were the marshal here to thank me:
The naming this commander doth confirm it.
Don Face! why he's the most authentic dealer
In these commodities, the superintendent
To all the quainter traffickers in town!...
Him will I prove, by a third person, to find
The subtleties of this dark labyrinth:
Which if I do discover, dear sir Mammon,
You'll give your poor friend leave, though no philosopher,
To laugh: for you that are, 'tis thought, shall weep.

    Face. Sir, he does pray, you'll not forget.

    Sur. I will not, sir.

Sir Epicure, I shall leave you.   *[Exit.*

    Mam. I follow you, straight.

    Face. But do so, good sir, to avoid suspicion.
This gentleman has a parlous head.

    Mam. But wilt thou, Ulen,
Be constant to thy promise?

    Face. As my life, sir.

    Mam. And wilt thou insinuate what I am, and praise
      me,
And say, I am a noble fellow?

    Face. O, what else, sir?
And that you'll make her royal with the stone,
An empress; and yourself, king of Bantam.

    Mam. Wilt thou do this?

    Face. Will I, sir!

    Mam. Lungs, my Lungs!
I love thee.

    Face. Send your stuff, sir, that my master
May busy himself about projection.

    Mam. Thou hast witch'd me, rogue: take, go.
                      [Gives him money.

    Face. Your jack, and all, sir.

Mam. Thou art a villain—I will send my jack,
And the weights too. Slave, I could bite thine ear.
Away, thou dost not care for me.

Face. Not I, sir!

Mam. Come, I was born to make thee, my good
weasel,
Set thee on a bench, and have thee twirl a chain
With the best lord's vermin of 'em all.

Face. Away, sir.

Mam. A count, nay, a count palatine—

Face. Good, sir, go.

Mam. Shall not advance thee better: no, nor faster.
                                              [*Exit.*

Re-enter SUBTLE *and* DOL.

Sub. Has he bit? has he bit?

Face. And swallow'd too, my Subtle.
I have given him line, and now he plays, i' faith.

Sub. And shall we twitch him?

Face. Thorough both the gills.
A wench is a rare bait, with which a man
No sooner's taken, but he straight firks mad.

Sub. Dol, my lord What'ts'hums sister, you must now
Bear your self *statelich.*

Dol. O let me alone.
I'll not forget my race, I warrant you.
I'll keep my distance, laugh and talk aloud;
Have all the tricks of a proud scurvy lady,
And be as rude as her woman.

Face. Well said, sanguine!

Sub. But will he send his andirons?

Face. His jack too,
And's iron shoeing-horn; I have spoke to him. Well,
I must not lose my wary gamester yonder.

Sub. O monsieur Caution, that *will not be gull'd.*

Face. Ay,
If I can strike a fine hook into him, now!—
The Temple-church, there I have cast mine angle.
Well, pray for me. I'll about it.   [*Knocking without.*

Sub. What, more gudgeons!

Dol, scout, scout! [DOL *goes to the window*.] Stay, Face,
    you must go to the door,

'Pray God it be my anabaptist.—Who is't, Dol?

  Dol. I know him not: he looks like a gold-end-man.

  Sub. 'Ods so! 'tis he, he said he would send what call
    you him?

The sanctified elder, that should deal

For Mammon's jack and andirons. Let him in.

Stay, help me off, first, with my gown. [*Exit* FACE *with
    the gown*.] Away,

Madam, to your withdrawing chamber. [*Exit* DOL.]
    Now,

In a new tune, new gesture, but old language.—

This fellow is sent from one negociates with me

About the stone too; for the holy brethren

Of Amsterdam, the exiled saints; that hope

To raise their discipline by it. I must use him

In some strange fashion, now, to make him admire me.—

Enter ANANIAS.

Where is my drudge?   [*Aloud.*

Re-enter FACE.

  Face. Sir!

  Sub. Take away the recipient,

And rectify your menstrue from the phlegma.

Then pour it on the Sol, in the cucurbite,

And let them macerate together.

  Face. Yes, sir.

And save the ground?

  Sub. No: *terra damnata*

Must not have entrance in the work.—Who are you?

  Ana. A faithful brother, if it please you.

  Sub. What's that?

A Lullianist? a Ripley? Filius artis?

Can you sublime and dulcify? calcine?

Know you the sapor pontic? sapor stiptic?

Or what is homogene, or heterogene?

Ana. I understand no heathen language, truly.

Sub. Heathen! you Knipper-doling? is Ars sacra,
Or chrysopœia, or spagyrica,
Or the pamphysic, or panarchic knowledge,
A heathen language?

Ana. Heathen Greek, I take it.

Sub. How! heathen Greek?

Ana. All's heathen but the Hebrew.

Sub. Sirrah, my varlet, stand you forth and speak to
      him,
Like a philosopher: answer, in the language.
Name the vexations, and the martyrizations
Of metals in the work.

Face. Sir, putrefaction,
Solution, ablution, sublimation,
Cohobation, calcination, ceration, and
Fixation.

Sub. This is heathen Greek, to you, now!—
And when comes vivification?

Face. After mortification.

Sub. What's cohobation?

Face. 'Tis the pouring on
Your aqua regis, and then drawing him off,
To the trine circle of the seven spheres.

Sub. What's the proper passion of metals?

Face. Malleation.

Sub. What's your *ultimum supplicium auri?*

Face. Antimonium.

Sub. This is heathen Greek to you!—And what's your
      mercury?

Face. A very fugitive, he will be gone, sir.

Sub. How know you him?

Face. By his viscosity,
His oleosity, and his suscitability.

Sub. How do you sublime him?

Face. With the calce of egg-shells,
White marble, talc.

Sub. Your magisterium, now,
What's that?

Face. Shifting, sir, your elements,
Dry into cold, cold into moist, moist into hot,
Hot into dry.

Sub. This is heathen Greek to you still!
Your *lapis philosophicus?*

Face. 'Tis a stone,
And not a stone; a spirit, a soul, and a body:
Which if you do dissolve, it is dissolv'd;
If you coagulate, it is coagulated;
If you make it to fly, it flieth.

Sub. Enough.   [*Exit* FACE.
This is heathen Greek to you! What are you, sir?

Ana. Please you, a servant of the exiled brethren,
That deal with widows and with orphans' goods;
And make a just account unto the saints:
A deacon.

Sub. O, you are sent from master Wholsome,
Your teacher?

Ana. From Tribulation Wholsome,
Our very zealous pastor.

Sub. Good! I have
Some orphans' goods to come here.

Ana. Of what kind, sir?

Sub. Pewter and brass, andirons and kitchen-
          ware,
Metals, that we must use our medicine on:
Wherein the brethren may have a pennyworth,
For ready money.

Ana. Were the orphans' parents
Sincere professors?

Sub. Why do you ask?

Ana. Because
We then are to deal justly, and give, in truth,
Their utmost value.

Sub. 'Slid, you'd cozen else,
And if their parents were not of the faithful!—
I will not trust you, now I think on it,
'Till I have talk'd with your pastor. Have you brought
          money

To buy more coals?

   Ana. No, surely.

   Sub. No! how so?

   Ana. The brethren bid me say unto you, sir,
Surely, they will not venture any more,
Till they may see projection.

   Sub. How!

   Ana. You have had,
For the instruments, as bricks, and loam, and glasses,
Already thirty pound; and for materials,
They say, some ninety more: and they have heard
    since,
That one, at Heidelberg, made it of an egg,
And a small paper of pin-dust.

   Sub. What's your name?

   Ana. My name is Ananias.

   Sub. Out, the varlet
That cozen'd the apostles! Hence, away!
Flee, mischief! had your holy consistory
No name to send me, of another sound,
Than wicked Ananias? send your elders
Hither, to make atonement for you, quickly,
And give me satisfaction; or out goes
The fire; and down th' alembecs, and the furnace,
Piger Henricus, or what not. Thou wretch!
Both sericon and bufo shall be lost,
Tell them. All hope of rooting out the bishops,
Or the antichristian hierarchy, shall perish,
If they stay threescore minutes: the aqueity,
Terreity, and sulphureity
Shall run together again, and all be annull'd,
Thou wicked Ananias! [*Exit* ANANIAS.] This will
    fetch 'em,
And make them haste towards their gulling more.
A man must deal like a rough nurse, and fright
Those that are froward, to an appetite.

Re-enter FACE *in his uniform, followed by* DRUGGER.

Face. He is busy with his spirits, but we'll upon him.

Sub. How now! what mates, what Baiards have we
    here?

Face. I told you, he would be furious.—Sir, here's
    Nab,
Has brought you another piece of gold to look on:
—We must appease him. Give it me,—and prays you,
You would devise—what is it, Nab?

Drug. A sign, sir.

Face. Ay, a good lucky one, a thriving sign, doctor.

Sub. I was devising now.

Face. 'Slight, do not say so,
He will repent he gave you any more—
What say you to his constellation, doctor,
The Balance?

Sub. No, that way is stale, and common.
A townsman born in Taurus, gives the bull,
Or the bull's-head: in Aries, the ram,
A poor-device! No, I will have his name
Form'd in some mystic character; whose radii,
Striking the senses of the passers by,
Shall, by a virtual influence, breed affections,
That may result upon the party owns it:
As thus—

Face. Nab!

Sub. He shall have *a bel*, that's *Abel;*
And by it standing one whose name is *Dee*,
In a *rug* gown, there's *D*, and *Rug*, that's *drug:*
And right anenst him a dog snarling *er;*
There's *Drugger*, Abel Drugger. That's his sign.
And here's now mystery and hieroglyphic!

Face. Abel, thou art made.

Drug. Sir, I do thank his worship.

Face. Six o' thy legs more will not do it, Nab.
He has brought you a pipe of tobacco, doctor.

Drug. Yes, sir:
I have another thing I would impart——

Face. Out with it, Nab.

Drug. Sir, there is lodged, hard by me,
A rich young widow——

Face. Good! a bona roba?

Drug. But nineteen, at the most.

Face. Very good, Abel.

Drug. Marry, she's not in fashion yet; she wears
A hood, but it stands a cop.

Face. No matter, Abel.

Drug. And I do now and then give her a fucus——

Face. What! dost thou deal, Nab?

Sub. I did tell you, captain.

Drug. And physic too, sometime, sir; for which she
    trusts me
With all her mind. She's come up here of purpose
To learn the fashion.

Face. Good (his match too!)—On, Nab.

Drug. And she does strangely long to know her
    fortune.

Face. 'Ods lid, Nab, send her to the doctor, hither.

Drug. Yes, I have spoke to her of his worship already;
But she's afraid it will be blown abroad,
And hurt her marriage.

Face. Hurt it! 'tis the way
To heal it, if 'twere hurt; to make it more
Follow'd and sought: Nab, thou shalt tell her this.
She'll be more known, more talk'd of; and your widows
Are ne'er of any price till they be famous;
Their honour is their multitude of suitors:
Send her, it may be thy good fortune. What!
Thou dost not know.

Drug. No, sir, she'll never marry
Under a knight: her brother has made a vow.

Face. What! and dost thou despair, my little Nab,
Knowing what the doctor has set down for thee,
And seeing so many of the city dubb'd?
One glass o' thy water, with a madam I know,
Will have it done, Nab: what's her brother, a knight?

Drug. No, sir, a gentleman newly warm in his land, sir,

Scarce cold in his one and twenty, that does govern
His sister here; and is a man himself
Of some three thousand a year, and is come up
To learn to quarrel, and to live by his wits,
And will go down again, and die in the country.

    Face. How! to quarrel?

    Drug. Yes, sir, to carry quarrels,
As gallants do; to manage them by line.

    Face. 'Slid, Nab, the doctor is the only man
In Christendom for him. He has made a table,
With mathematical demonstrations,
Touching the art of quarrels: he will give him
An instrument to quarrel by. Go, bring them both,
Him and his sister. And, for thee, with her
The doctor happ'ly may persuade. Go to:
'Shalt give his worship a new damask suit
Upon the premises.

    Sub. O, good captain!

    Face. He shall;
He is the honestest fellow, doctor.—Stay not,
No offers; bring the damask, and the parties.

    Drug. I'll try my power, sir.

    Face. And thy will too, Nab.

    Sub. 'Tis good tobacco, this! what is't an ounce?

    Face. He'll send you a pound, doctor.

    Sub. O, no.

    Face. He will do't.
It is the goodest soul!—Abel, about it.
Thou shalt know more anon. Away, be gone.—

                [Exit ABEL.

A miserable rogue, and lives with cheese,
And has the worms. That was the cause, indeed,
Why he came now: he dealt with me in private,
To get a med'cine for them.

    Sub. And shall, sir. This works.

    Face. A wife, a wife for one of us, my dear Subtle!
We'll e'en draw lots, and he that fails, shall have
The more in goods....

    Sub. Rather the less: for she may be so light

She may want grains.
    Face. Ay, or be such a burden,
A man would scarce endure her for the whole.
    Sub. Faith, best let's see her first, and then determine.
    Face. Content: but Dol must have no breath on't.
    Sub. Mum.
Away you, to your Surly yonder, catch him.
    Face. 'Pray God I have not staid too long.
    Sub. I fear it.   [*Exeunt.*

ACT THE THIRD

SCENE I: The Lane before LOVEWIT's House.

Enter TRIBULATION WHOLESOME, *and* ANANIAS.

Tri. These chastisements are common to the saints,
And such rebukes we of the separation
Must bear with willing shoulders, as the trials
Sent forth to tempt our frailties.

Ana. In pure zeal,
I do not like the man, he is a heathen,
And speaks the language of Canaan, truly.

Tri. I think him a profane person indeed.

Ana. He bears
The visible mark of the beast in his forehead.
And for his stone, it is a work of darkness,
And with philosophy blinds the eyes of man.

Tri. Good brother, we must bend unto all means,
That may give furtherance to the holy cause.

Ana. Which his cannot: the sanctified cause
Should have a sanctified course.

Tri. Not always necessary:
The children of perdition are oft-times
Made instruments even of the greatest works:
Beside, we should give somewhat to man's nature,
The place he lives in, still about the fire,
And fume of metals, that intoxicate
The brain of man, and make him prone to passion.
Where have you greater atheists than your cooks?
Or more profane, or choleric, than your glass-men?
More antichristian than your bell-founders?
What makes the devil so devilish, I would ask you,
Sathan, our common enemy, but his being
Perpetually about the fire, and boiling
Brimstone and arsenic? We must give, I say,
Unto the motives, and the stirrers up

Of humours in the blood. It may be so,
When as the work is done, the stone is made,
This heat of his may turn into a zeal,
And stand up for the beauteous discipline,...
We must await his calling, and the coming
Of the good spirit. You did fault, t' upbraid him
With the brethren's blessing of Heidelberg, weighing
What need we have to hasten on the work,
For the restoring of the silenced saints,
Which ne'er will be, but by the philosopher's stone.
And so a learned elder, one of Scotland,
Assured me; *aurum potabile* being
The only med'cine, for the civil magistrate,
T' incline him to a feeling of the cause;
And must be daily used in the disease.

   Ana. I have not edified more, truly, by man;
Not since the beautiful light first shone on me:
And I am sad my zeal hath so offended.

   Tri. Let us call on him then.

   Ana. The motion's good,
And of the spirit; I will knock first. [*Knocks.*] Peace be
     within!   [*The door is opened, and they enter.*

SCENE II: A Room in LOVEWIT'S House.

Enter SUBTLE, *followed by* TRIBULATION *and*
ANANIAS.

   Sub. O, are you come? 'twas time. Your threescore
     minutes
Were at last thread, you see; and down had gone
Furnus acediæ, turris circulatorius:
Lembec, bolt's-head, retort and pelican
Had all been cinders.—Wicked Ananias!
Art thou return'd? nay then, it goes down yet.

   Tri. Sir, be appeased; he is come to humble
Himself in spirit, and to ask your patience,
If too much zeal hath carried him aside
From the due path.

Sub. Why, this doth qualify!

Tri. The brethren had no purpose, verily,
To give you the least grievance: but are ready
To lend their willing hands to any project
The spirit and you direct.

Sub. This qualifies more!

Tri. And for the orphans' goods, let them be valued,
Or what is needful else to the holy work,
It shall be numbered; here, by me, the saints,
Throw down their purse before you.

Sub. This qualifies most!
Why, thus it should be, now you understand.
Have I discours'd so unto you of our stone,
And of the good that it shall bring your cause?
Shew'd you (beside the main of hiring forces
Abroad, drawing the Hollanders, your friends,
From the Indies, to serve you, with all their fleet)
That even the med'cinal use shall make you a faction,
And party in the realm? As, put the case,
That some great man in state, he have the gout,
Why, you but send three drops of your elixir,
You help him straight: there you have made a friend.
Another has the palsy or the dropsy,
He takes of your incombustible stuff,
He's young again: ...A lord that is a leper,
A knight that has the bone-ache, or a squire
That hath both these, you make them smooth and
        sound,
With a bare fricace of your med'cine: still
You increase your friends.

Tri. Ay, it is very pregnant.

Sub. And then the turning of this lawyer's pewter
To plate at Christmas.——

Ana. Christ-tide, I pray you.

Sub. Yet, Ananias!

Ana. I have done.

Sub. Or changing
His parcel gilt to massy gold. You cannot
But raise you friends. Withal, to be of power

To pay an army in the field, to buy
The king of France out of his realms, or Spain
Out of his Indies. What can you not do
Against lords spiritual or temporal,
That shall oppone you?

 Tri. Verily, 'tis true.
We may be temporal lords ourselves, I take it.

 Sub. You may be any thing, and leave off to make
Long-winded exercises; or suck up
Your *ha!* and *hum!* in a tune. I not deny,
But such as are not graced in a state,
May, for their ends, be adverse in religion,
And get a tune to call the flock together:
For, to say sooth, a tune does much with women,
And other phlegmatic people; it is your bell.

 Ana. Bells are profane; a tune may be religious.

 Sub. No warning with you! then farewell my patience.
'Slight, it shall down: I will not be thus tortured.

 Tri. I pray you, sir.

 Sub. All shall perish. I have spoke it.

 Tri. Let me find grace, sir, in your eyes; the man
He stands corrected: neither did his zeal,
But as yourself, allow a tune somewhere.
Which now, being tow'rd the stone, we shall not
  need.

 Sub. No, nor your holy vizard, to win widows
To give you legacies; or make zealous wives
To rob their husbands for the common cause:
Nor take the start of bonds broke but one day,
And say, they were forfeited by providence.
Nor shall you need o'er night to eat huge meals,
To celebrate your next day's fast...Nor cast
Before your hungry hearers scrupulous bones;
As whether a Christian may hawk or hunt,
Or whether matrons of the holy assembly
May lay their hair out, or wear doublets,
Or have that idol starch about their linen.

 Ana. It is indeed an idol.

 Tri. Mind him not, sir.

I do command thee, spirit of zeal, but trouble,
To peace within him! Pray you, sir, go on.
  Sub. Nor shall you need to libel 'gainst the prelates,
And shorten so your ears against the hearing
Of the next wire-drawn grace. Nor of necessity
Rail against plays, to please the alderman
Whose daily custard you devour: nor lie
With zealous rage till you are hoarse. Not one
Of these so singular arts. Nor call your selves
By names of Tribulation, Persecution,
Restraint, Long-patience, and such like, affected
By the whole family or wood of you,
Only for glory, and to catch the ear
Of the disciple.
  Tri. Truly, sir, they are
Ways that the godly brethren have invented,
For propagation of the glorious cause,
As very notable means, and whereby also
Themselves grow soon, and profitably, famous.
  Sub. O, but the stone, all's idle to it! nothing!
The art of angels, nature's miracle,
The divine secret that doth fly in clouds
From east to west; and whose tradition
Is not from men, but spirits.
  Ana. I hate traditions;
I do not trust them.——
  Tri. Peace!
  Ana. They are popish all.
I will not peace: I will not——
  Tri. Ananias!
  Ana. Please the profane, to grieve the godly; I may
    not.
  Sub. Well, Ananias, thou shalt overcome.
  Tri. It is an ignorant zeal that haunts him, sir:
But truly, else, a very faithful brother,
A botcher, and a man, by revelation,
That hath a competent knowledge of the truth.
  Sub. Has he a competent sum there in the bag
To buy the goods within? I am made guardian,

And must, for charity, and conscience sake,
Now see the most be made for my poor orphan;
Though I desire the brethren too good gainers:
There they are within. When you have view'd, and
          bought 'em,
And ta'en the inventory of what they are,
They are ready for projection; there's no more
To do: cast on the med'cine, so much silver
As there is tin there, so much gold as brass,
I'll give't you in by weight.
   Tri. But how long time,
Sir, must the saints expect yet?
   Sub. Let me see,
How's the moon now? Eight, nine, ten days hence,
He will be silver potate; then three days
Before he citronise: Some fifteen days,
The magisterium will be perfected.
   Ana. About the second day of the third week,
In the ninth month?
   Sub. Yes, my good Ananias.
   Tri. What will the orphan's goods arise to, think you?
   Sub. Some hundred marks, as much as fill'd three
          cars,
Unladed now: you'll make six millions of them.—
But I must have more coals laid in.
   Tri. How!
   Sub. Another load,
And then we have finish'd. We must now increase
Our fire to *ignis ardens*, we are past
Fimus equinus, balnei, cineris,
And all those lenter heats. If the holy purse
Should with this draught fall low, and that the saints
Do need a present sum, I have a trick
To melt the pewter, you shall buy now, instantly,
And with a tincture make you as good Dutch dollars
As any are in Holland.
   Tri. Can you so?
   Sub. Ay, and shall 'bide the third examination.
   Ana. It will be joyful tidings to the brethren.

Sub. But you must carry it secret.

Tri. Ay; but stay,
This act of coining, is it lawful?

Ana. Lawful!
We know no magistrate: or, if we did,
This is foreign coin.

Sub. It is no coining, sir.
It is but casting.

Tri. Ha! you distinguish well:
Casting of money may be lawful.

Ana. 'Tis, sir.

Tri. Truly, I take it so.

Sub. There is no scruple,
Sir, to be made of it; believe Ananias:
This case of conscience he is studied in.

Tri. I'll make a question of it to the brethren.

Ana. The brethren shall approve it lawful, doubt not.
Where shall it be done?   [*Knocking without.*

Sub. For that we'll talk anon.
There's some to speak with me. Go in, I pray you,
And view the parcels. That's the inventory.
I'll come to you straight. [*Exeunt* TRIB. *and* ANA.]
    Who is it?—Face! appear.

Enter FACE *in his uniform.*

How now! good prize?

Face. Good pox! yond' costive cheater
Never came on.

Sub. How then?

Face. I have walk'd the round
Till now, and no such thing.

Sub. And have you quit him?

Face. Quit him! an hell would quit him too, he were
    happy.
Slight! would you have me stalk like a mill-jade,
All day, for one that will not yield us grains?
I know him of old.

Sub. O, but to have gull'd him,
Had been a mastery.

Face. Let him go, black boy!
And turn thee, that some fresh news may possess thee.
A noble count, a don of Spain, my dear
Delicious compeer, and my party-bawd,
Who is come hither private for his conscience,
And brought munition with him, six great slops,
Bigger than three Dutch hoys, beside round trunks,
Furnished with pistolets, and pieces of eight,
Will straight be here, my rogue, to have thy bath,
(That is the colour,) and to make his battery
Upon our Dol, our castle, our cinque-port,
Our Dover pier, our what thou wilt. Where is she?
She must prepare perfumes, delicate linen,
The bath in chief, a banquet, and her wit...
Where is the doxy?
    Sub. I'll send her to thee:
And but dispatch my brace of little John Leydens,
And come again my self.
    Face. Are they within then?
    Sub. Numbering the sum.
    Face. How much?
    Sub. A hundred marks, boy.   [*Exit.*
    Face. Why, this is a lucky day. Ten pounds of
        Mammon!
Three of my clerk! a portague of my grocer!
This of the brethren! beside reversions,
And states to come in the widow, and my count!
My share to-day will not be bought for forty—

                    Enter DOL.

    Dol. What?
    Face. Pounds, dainty Dorothy! art thou so near?
    Dol. Yes; say, lord general, how fares our camp?
    Face. As with the few that had entrench'd them-
        selves
Safe, by their discipline, against a world, Dol,
And laugh'd within those trenches, and grew fat
With thinking on the booties, Dol, brought in
Daily by their small parties. This dear hour,

A doughty don is taken with my Dol;
And thou mayst make his ransom what thou wilt....
   Dol. What is he, general?
   Face. An adalantado,
A grandee, girl. Was not my Dapper here yet?
   Dol. No.
   Face. Nor my Drugger?
   Dol. Neither.
   Face. A pox on 'em,
They are so long a furnishing! such stinkards
Would not be seen upon these festival days.—

        Re-enter SUBTLE.

How now! have you done?
   Sub. Done. They are gone: the sum
Is here in bank, my Face. I would we knew
Another chapman now would buy 'em outright.
   Face. 'Slid, Nab shall do't against he have the widow
To furnish household.
   Sub. Excellent, well thought on:
Pray God he come.
   Face. I pray he keep away
Till our new business be o'erpast.
   Sub. But, Face,
How cam'st thou by this secret don?
   Face. A spirit
Brought me th' intelligence in a paper here,
As I was conjuring yonder in my circle
For Surly; I have my flies abroad. Your bath
Is famous, Subtle, by my means....His great
Verdugoship has not a jot of language;
So much the easier to be cozen'd, my Dolly.
He will come here in a hired coach, obscure,
And our own coachman, whom I have sent as guide,
No creature else. [*Knocking without.*] Who's that?
                         [*Exit* DOL.

   Sub. It is not he?
   Face. O no, not yet this hour.

Re-enter DOL.

Sub. Who is't?

Dol. Dapper,
Your clerk.

Face. God's will then, queen of Fairy,
On with your tire; [*Exit* DOL.] and, doctor, with your
    robes.
Let's dispatch him for God's sake.

Sub. 'Twill be long.

Face. I warrant you, take but the cues I give you,
It shall be brief enough. [*Goes to the window.*] 'Slight,
    here are more!
Abel, and I think the angry boy, the heir,
That fain would quarrel.

Sub. And the widow?

Face. No,
Not that I see. Away!   [*Exit* SUB.

Enter DAPPER.

                    —O sir, you are welcome.
The doctor is within a moving for you;
I have had the most ado to win him to it!—
He swears you'll be the darling of the dice:
He never heard her highness dote till now.
Your aunt has given you the most gracious words
That can be thought on.

Dap. Shall I see her grace?

Face. See her, and kiss her too.—

Enter ABEL, *followed by* KASTRIL.

                    What, honest Nab!
Hast brought the damask?

Nab. No, sir; here's tobacco.

Face. 'Tis well done, Nab: thou'lt bring the damask
    too?

Drug. Yes: here's the gentleman, captain, master
    Kastril,
I have brought to see the doctor.

Face. Where's the widow?

Drug. Sir, as he likes, his sister, he says, shall come.

Face. O, is it so? good time. Is your name Kastril, sir?

Kas. Ay, and the best of the Kastrils, I'd be sorry else,
By fifteen hundred a year. Where is the doctor?
My mad tobacco-boy, here, tells me of one
That can do things: has he any skill?

Face. Wherein, sir?

Kas. To carry a business, manage a quarrel fairly,
Upon fit terms.

Face. It seems, sir, you are but young
About the town, that can make that a question.

Kas. Sir, not so young, but I have heard some speech
Of the angry boys, and seen them take tobacco;
And in his shop; and I can take it too.
And I would fain be one of 'em, and go down
And practise in the country.

Face. Sir, for the duello,
The doctor, I assure you, shall inform you,
To the least shadow of a hair; and shew you
An instrument he has of his own making,
Wherewith no sooner shall you make report
Of any quarrel, but he will take the height on't
Most instantly, and tell in what degree
Of safety it lies in, or mortality.
And how it may be borne, whether in a right line,
Or a half circle; or may else be cast
Into an angle blunt, if not acute:
All this he will demonstrate. And then, rules
To give and take the lie by.

Kas. How! to take it?

Face. Yes, in oblique he'll shew you, or in circle;
But never in diameter. The whole town
Study his theorems, and dispute them ordinarily
At the eating academies.

Kas. But does he teach
Living by the wits too?

Face. Any thing whatever.
You cannot think that subtlety but he reads it.

He made me a captain. I was a stark pimp,
Just of your standing, 'fore I met with him;
It is not two months since. I'll tell you his method:
First, he will enter you at some ordinary.
   Kas. No, I'll not come there: you shall pardon me.
   Face. For why, sir?
   Kas. There's gaming there, and tricks.
   Face. Why, would you be
A gallant, and not game?
   Kas. Ay, 'twill spend a man.
   Face. Spend you! it will repair you when you are
     spent:
How do they live by their wits there, that have vented
Six times your fortunes?
   Kas. What, three thousand a year!
   Face. Ay, forty thousand.
   Kas. Are there such?
   Face. Ay, sir,
And gallants yet. Here's a young gentleman
Is born to nothing,—[*Points to* DAPPER.] forty marks a
    year,
Which I count nothing:—he is to be initiated,
And have a fly of the doctor. He will win you,
By unresistible luck, within this fortnight,
Enough to buy a barony. They will set him
Upmost, at the groom porters, all the Christmas:
And for the whole year through, at every place,
Where there is play, present him with the chair;
The best attendance, the best drink; sometimes
Two glasses of Canary, and pay nothing;
The purest linen, and the sharpest knife....
You shall have your ordinaries bid for him,
As play-houses for a poet; and the master
Pray him aloud to name what dish he affects,
Which must be butter'd shrimps: and those that drink
To no mouth else, will drink to his, as being
The goodly president mouth of all the board.
   Kas. Do you not gull one?
   Face. 'Ods my life! do you think it?

You shall have a cast commander, (can but get
In credit with a glover, or a spurrier,
For some two pair of either's ware aforehand,)
Will, by most swift posts, dealing [but] with him,
Arrive at competent means to keep himself,. . .
And be admired for't.

    Kas. Will the doctor teach this?

    Face. He will do more, sir: when your land is gone,
As men of spirit hate to keep earth long,
In a vacation, when small money is stirring,
And ordinaries suspended till the term,
He'll shew a perspective, where on one side
You shall behold the faces and the persons
Of all sufficient young heirs in town,
Whose bonds are current for commodity;
On th' other side, the merchants' forms, and others,
That without help of any second broker,
Who would expect a share, will trust such parcels:
In the third square, the very street and sign
Where the commodity dwells, and does but wait
To be deliver'd, be it pepper, soap,
Hops, or tobacco, oat-meal, woad, or cheeses.
All which you may so handle, to enjoy
To your own use, and never stand obliged.

    Kas. I'faith! is he such a fellow?

    Face. Why, Nab here knows him.
And then for making matches for rich widows,
Young gentlewomen, heirs, the fortunat'st man!
He's sent to, far and near, all over England,
To have his counsel, and to know their fortunes.

    Kas. God's will, my suster shall see him.

    Face. I'll tell you, sir,
What he did tell me of Nab. It's a strange thing!—
By the way, you must eat no cheese, Nab, it breeds
    melancholy,
And that same melancholy breeds worms; but pass it:—
He told me, honest Nab here was ne'er at tavern
But once in's life.

    Drug. Truth, and no more I was not.

Face. And then he was so sick——
Drug. Could he tell you that too?
Face. How should I know it?
Drug. In troth we had been a shooting,
And had a piece of fat ram-mutton to supper,
That lay so heavy o' my stomach——
Face. And he has no head
To bear any wine; for what with the noise of the fidlers,
And care of his shop, for he dares keep no servants——
Drug. My head did so ach——
Face. And he was fain to be brought home,
The doctor told me: and then a good old woman——
Drug. Yes, faith, she dwells in Sea-coal-lane,—did cure
    me,
With sodden ale, and pellitory of the wall;
Cost me but two-pence. I had another sickness
Was worse than that.
Face. Ay, that was with the grief
Thou took'st for being cess'd at eighteen-pence,
For the water-work.
Drug. In truth, and it was like
T' have cost me almost my life.
Face. Thy hair went off?
Drug. Yes, sir; 'twas done for spite.
Face. Nay, so says the doctor.
Kas. Pray thee, tobacco-boy, go fetch my suster;
I'll see this learned boy before I go;
And so shall she.
Face. Sir, he is busy now:
But if you have a sister to fetch hither,
Perhaps your own pains may command her sooner;
And he by that time will be free.
Kas. I go.   [*Exit*.
Face. Drugger, she's thine: the damask!—[*Exit*
    ABEL.] Subtle and I
Must wrestle for her. [*Aside*.]—Come on, master Dapper,
You see how I turn clients here away,
To give your cause dispatch: have you perform'd
The ceremonies were enjoin'd you?

Dap. Yes, of the vinegar,
And the clean shirt.

Face. 'Tis well: that shirt may do you
More worship than you think. Your aunt's a-fire,
But that she will not shew it, t' have a sight of you.
Have you provided for her grace's servants?

Dap. Yes, here are six score Edward shillings.

Face. Good!

Dap. And an old Harry's sovereign.

Face. Very good!

Dap. And three James shillings, and an Elizabeth
groat,
Just twenty nobles.

Face. O, you are too just.
I would you had had the other noble in Maries.

Dap. I have some Philip and Maries.

Face. Ay, those same
Are best of all: where are they? Hark, the doctor.

Enter SUBTLE, *disguised like a priest of Fairy, with a
stripe of cloth.*

Sub. [*In a feigned voice.*] Is yet her grace's cousin
come?

Face. He is come.

Sub. And is he fasting?

Face. Yes.

Sub. And hath cried hum?

Face. Thrice, you must answer.

Dap. Thrice.

Sub. And as oft buz?

Face. If you have, say.

Dap. I have.

Sub. Then, to her cuz,
Hoping that he hath vinegar'd his senses,
As he was bid, the Fairy queen dispenses,
By me, this robe, the petticoat of fortune;
Which that he straight put on, she doth importune.
And though to fortune near be her petticoat,
Yet nearer is her smock, the queen doth note:

And therefore, ev'n of that a piece she hath sent,
Which, being a child, to wrap him in was rent;
And prays him for a scarf he now will wear it,
With as much love as then her grace did tear it,
About his eyes, [*They blind him with the rag.*] to shew he
    is fortunate.
And, trusting unto her to make his state,
He'll throw away all worldly pelf about him;
Which that he will perform, she doth not doubt him.
   Face. She need not doubt him, sir. Alas, he has
    nothing,
But what he will part withal as willingly,
Upon her grace's word—throw away your purse—
As she would ask it:—handkerchiefs and all—
                  [*He throws away, as they bid him.*
She cannot bid that thing, but he'll obey.—
If you have a ring about you, cast it off,
Or a silver seal at your wrist; her grace will send
Her fairies here to search you, therefore deal
Directly with her highness: if they find
That you conceal a mite, you are undone.
   Dap. Truly, there's all.
   Face. All what?
   Dap. My money; truly.
   Face. Keep nothing that is transitory about you.
Bid Dol play music. [*Aside to* SUBTLE.]—Look, the elves
    are come   [DOL *plays on the cittern within.*
To pinch you, if you tell not truth. Advise you.
                           [*They pinch him.*
   Dap. O! I have a paper with a spur-ryal in't.
   Face. *Ti, ti.*
They knew't, they say.
   Sub. Ti, ti, ti, ti. He has more yet.
   Face. Ti, ti-ti-ti. In the other pocket?
                            [*Aside to* SUB.
   Sub. *Titi, titi, titi, titi, titi.*
They must pinch him or he will never confess, they say.
                        [*They pinch him again.*
   Dap. O, O!

Face. Nay, pray you hold: he is her grace's nephew,
Ti, ti, ti? What care you? good faith, you shall care.—
Deal plainly, sir, and shame the fairies. Shew
You are innocent.

Dap. By this good light, I have nothing.

Sub. Ti, ti, ti, ti, to, ta. He does equivocate, she says:
Ti, ti do ti, ti ti do, ti da; and swears by the *light* when
  he is blinded.

Dap. By this good *dark*, I have nothing but a half-
  crown
Of gold about my wrist, that my love gave me;
And a leaden heart I wore since she forsook me.

Face. I thought 'twas something. And would you
  incur
Your aunt's displeasure for these trifles? Come,
I had rather you had thrown away twenty half-crowns.
                                        [*Takes it off.*
You may wear your leaden heart still.—

Enter DOL *hastily.*

                    How now!

Sub. What news, Dol?

Dol. Yonder's your knight, sir Mammon.

Face. 'Ods lid, we never thought of him till now!
Where is he?

Dol. Here hard by: he is at the door.

Sub. And you are not ready, now! Dol, get his suit.
                                        [*Exit* DOL.
He must not be sent back.

Face. O by no means.
What shall we do with this same puffin here,
Now he's on the spit?

Sub. Why, lay him back awhile,
With some device.

Re-enter DOL *with Face's clothes.*

—*Ti, ti, ti, ti, ti, ti,* Would her grace speak with me?
I come.—Help, Dol!   [*Knocking without.*

Face. [*Speaks through the key-hole.*] Who's there?
    sir Epicure,
My master's in the way. Please you to walk
Three or four turns, but till his back be turn'd,
And I am for you.—Quickly, Dol!

Sub. Her grace
Commends her kindly to you, master Dapper.

Dap. I long to see her grace.

Sub. She now is set
At dinner in her bed, and she has sent you
From her own private trencher, a dead mouse,
And a piece of gingerbread, to be merry withal,
And stay your stomach, lest you faint with fasting:
Yet if you could hold out till she saw you, she says,
It would be better for you.

Face. Sir, he shall
Hold out, an 'twere this two hours, for her highness;
I can assure you that. We will not lose
All we have done.——

Sub. He must not see, nor speak
To any body, till then.

Face. For that we'll put, sir,
A stay in's mouth.

Sub. Of what?

Face. Of gingerbread.
Make you it fit. He that hath pleas'd her grace
Thus far, shall not now crincle for a little.—
Gape sir, and let him fit you.

       [*They thrust a gag of gingerbread in his mouth.*

Sub. Where shall we now
Bestow him?

Dol. In the privy.

Sub. Come along, sir,
I now must shew you Fortune's privy lodgings.

Face. Are they perfum'd, and his bath ready?

Sub. All:
Only the fumigation's somewhat strong.

Face. [*speaking through the key-hole.*] Sir Epicure, I am
    yours, sir, by and by.   [*Exeunt with* DAPPER

ACT THE FOURTH

Scene I: A Room in Lovewit's House.

Enter Face and Mammon.

Face. O sir, you are come in the only finest time.——
Mam. Where's master?
Face. Now preparing for projection, sir.
Your stuff will be all changed shortly.
Mam. Into gold?
Face. To gold and silver, sir.
Mam. Silver I care not for.
Face. Yes, sir, a little to give beggars.
Mam. Where's the lady?
Face. At hand here. I have told her such brave things
   of you,
Touching your bounty, and your noble spirit——
Mam. Hast thou?
Face. As she is almost in her fit to see you.
But, good sir, no divinity in your conference,
For fear of putting her in rage.——
Mam. I warrant thee.
Face. Six men [sir] will not hold her down: and then,
If the old man should hear or see you——
Mam. Fear not.
Face. The very house, sir, would run mad. You
   know it,
How scrupulous he is, and violent,
'Gainst the least act of sin. Physic, or mathematics,
Poetry, state, or bawdry, as I told you,
She will endure, and never startle; but
No word of controversy.
Mam. I am school'd, good Ulen.
Face. And you must praise her house, remember that,
And her nobility.
Mam. Let me alone:

No herald, no, nor antiquary, Lungs,
Shall do it better. Go.
   Face. Why, this is yet
A kind of modern happiness, to have
Dol Common for a great lady.   [*Aside, and exit.*
   Mam. Now, Epicure,
Heighten thy self, talk to her all in gold;
Rain her as many showers as Jove did drops
Unto his Danäe; shew the god a miser,
Compared with Mammon. What! the stone will do't.
She shall feel gold, taste gold...I will be puissant,
And mighty in my talk to her.—

     Re-enter FACE *with* DOL *richly dressed.*

                       Here she comes.
   Face. To him, Dol, suckle him.—This is the noble
    knight,
I told your ladyship—
   Mam. Madam, with your pardon,
I kiss your vesture.
   Dol. Sir, I were uncivil
If I would suffer that; my lip to you, sir.
   Mam. I hope my lord your brother be in health, lady.
   Dol. My lord, my brother is, though I no lady, sir.
   Face. Well said, my Guinea bird.   [*Aside.*
   Mam. Right noble madam—
   Face. O, we shall have most fierce idolatry.   [*Aside.*
   Mam. 'Tis your prerogative.
   Dol. Rather your courtesy.
   Mam. Were there nought else t' enlarge your virtues
    to me,
These answers speak your breeding, and your blood.
   Dol. Blood we boast none, sir, a poor baron's daughter.
   Mam. Poor! and gat you? profane not....
   Dol. Sir, although
We may be said to want the gilt and trappings,
The dress of honour, yet we strive to keep
The seeds and the materials.
   Mam. I do see

The old ingredient, virtue, was not lost,
Nor the drug money used to make your compound.
There is a strange nobility in your eye,
This lip, that chin! methinks you do resemble
One of the Austriac princes.

   Face. Very like!
Her father was an Irish costarmonger.   [*Aside.*

   Mam. The house of Valois just had such a nose,
And such a forehead yet the Medici
Of Florence boast.

   Dol. Troth, and I have been liken'd
To all these princes.

   Face. I'll be sworn, I heard it.

   Mam. I know not how! it is not any one,
But e'en the very choice of all their features.

   Face. I'll in, and laugh.   [*Aside and exit.*

   Mam. A certain touch, or air,
That sparkles a divinity, beyond
An earthly beauty!

   Dol. O, you play the courtier.

   Mam. Good lady, give me leave——

   Dol. In faith, I may not,
To mock me, sir.

   Mam. To burn in this sweet flame;
The phœnix never knew a nobler death.

   Dol. Nay, now you court the courtier, and destroy
What you would build: this art, sir, in your words,
Calls your whole faith in question.

   Mam. By my soul——

   Dol. Nay, oaths are made of the same air, sir.

   Mam. Nature
Never bestow'd upon mortality
A more unblamed, a more harmonious feature;
She play'd the step-dame in all faces else:
Sweet madam, let me be particular——

   Dol. Particular, sir! I pray you know your distance.

   Mam. In no ill sense, sweet lady; but to ask
How your fair graces pass the hours? I see
You are lodg'd here, in the house of a rare man,

An excellent artist; but what's that to you?

   Dol. Yes, sir; I study here the mathematics,
And distillation.

   Mam. O, I cry your pardon.
He's a divine instructor! can extract
The souls of all things by his art; call all
The virtues, and the miracles of the sun,
Into a temperate furnace; teach dull nature
What her own forces are. A man, the emperor
Has courted above Kelly; sent his medals
And chains, to invite him.

   Dol. Ay, and for his physic, sir——

   Mam. Above the art of Æsculapius,
That drew the envy of the thunderer!
I know all this, and more.

   Dol. Troth, I am taken, sir,
Whole with these studies, that contemplate nature.

   Mam. It is a noble humour; but this form
Was not intended to so dark a use.
Had you been crooked, foul, of some coarse mould,
A cloister had done well; but such a feature
That might stand up the glory of a kingdom,
To live recluse! is a mere solœcism,
Though in a nunnery. It must not be.
I muse, my lord your brother will permit it:
You should spend half my land first, were I he.
Does not this diamond better on my finger,
Than in the quarry?

   Dol. Yes.

   Mam. Why, you are like it.
You were created, lady, for the light.
Here, you shall wear it; take it, the first pledge
Of what I speak, to bind you to believe me.

   Dol. In chains of adamant?

   Mam. Yes, the strongest bands.
And take a secret too—here, by your side,
Doth stand this hour, the happiest man in Europe.

   Dol. You are contented, sir?

   Mam. Nay, in true being.

The envy of princes and the fear of states.

   Dol. Say you so, sir Epicure?

   Mam. Yes, and thou shalt prove it,
Daughter of honour. I have cast mine eye
Upon thy form, and I will rear this beauty
Above all styles.

   Dol. You mean no treason, sir?

   Mam. No, I will take away that jealousy.
I am the lord of the philosopher's stone,
And thou the lady.

   Dol. How, sir! have you that?

   Mam. I am the master of the mastery.
This day the good old wretch here o' the house
Has made it for us: now he's at projection.
Think therefore thy first wish now, let me hear it;
And it shall rain into thy lap, no shower,
But floods of gold, whole cataracts, a deluge,
To get a nation on thee.

   Dol. You are pleased, sir,
To work on the ambition of our sex.

   Mam. I am pleased the glory of her sex should know,
This nook, here, of the Friers is no climate
For her to live obscurely in, to learn
Physic and surgery, for the constable's wife
Of some odd hundred in Essex; but come forth,
And taste the air of palaces; eat, drink
The toils of empirics, and their boasted practice;
Tincture of pearl, and coral, gold and amber;
Be seen at feasts and triumphs; have it ask'd,
What miracle she is? set all the eyes
Of court a-fire, like a burning glass,
And work them into cinders, when the jewels
Of twenty states adorn thee, and the light
Strikes out the stars! that, when thy name is mention'd,
Queens may look pale; and we but shewing our love,
Nero's Poppæa may be lost in story!
Thus will we have it.

   Dol. I could well consent, sir.
But, in a monarchy, how will this be?

The prince will soon take notice, and both seize
You and your stone, it being a wealth unfit
For any private subject.

   Mam. If he knew it.

   Dol. Yourself do boast it, sir.

   Mam. To thee, my life.

   Dol. O, but beware, sir! you may come to end
The remnant of your days in a loth'd prison,
By speaking of it.

   Mam. 'Tis no idle fear:
We'll therefore go withal, my girl, and live
In a free state, where we will eat our mullets,
Soused in high-country wines, sup pheasants eggs,
And have our cockles boil'd in silver shells;
Our shrimps to swim again, as when they liv'd,
In a rare butter made of dolphins milk,
Whose cream does look like opals;...
   ... And thou shalt have thy wardrobe
Richer than nature's, still to change thy self,
And vary oftener, for thy pride, than she,
Or art, her wise and almost-equal servant.

Re-enter FACE.

   Face. Sir, you are too loud. I hear you every word
Into the laboratory. Some fitter place;
The garden, or great chamber above. How like you her?

   Mam. Excellent! Lungs. There's for thee.

[*Gives him money.*

   Face. But do you hear?
Good sir, beware, no mention of the rabins.

   Mam. We think not on 'em. [*Exeunt* MAM. *and* DOL.

   Face. O, it is well, sir.—Subtle!

Enter SUBTLE.

Dost thou not laugh?

   Sub. Yes; are they gone?

   Face. All's clear.

   Sub. The widow is come.

   Face. And your quarrelling disciple?

Sub. Ay.

Face. I must to my captainship again then.

Sub. Stay, bring them in first.

Face. So I meant. What is she?
A bonnibel?

Sub. I know not.

Face. We'll draw lots:
You'll stand to that?

Sub. What else?

Face. O, for a suit,
To fall now like a curtain, flap!

Sub. To the door, man.

Face. You'll have the first kiss, 'cause I am not ready.
[*Exit.*

Sub. Yes, and perhaps hit you through both the
nostrils.

Face. [*within.*] Who would you speak with?

Kas. [*within.*] Where's the captain?

Face. [*within.*] Gone, sir.
About some business.

Kas. [*within.*] Gone!

Face. [*within.*] He'll return straight.
But master doctor, his lieutenant, is here.

Enter KASTRIL, *followed by* Dame PLIANT.

Sub. Come near, my worshipful boy, my *terræ fili*,
That is, my boy of land; make thy approaches:
Welcome; I know thy lusts, and thy desires,
And I will serve and satisfy them. Begin,
Charge me from thence, or thence, or in this line;
Here is my centre: ground thy quarrel.

Kas. You lie.

Sub. How, child of wrath and anger! the loud lie?
For what, my sudden boy?

Kas. Nay, that look you to,
I am afore-hand.

Sub. O, this is no true grammar,
And as ill logic! You must render causes, child,
Your first and second intentions, know your canons

And your divisions, moods, degrees, and differences,
Your predicaments, substance, and accident,
Series extern and intern, with their causes,
Efficient, material, formal, final,
And have your elements perfect?

    Kas. What is this!
The angry tongue he talks in?   [*Aside.*

    Sub. That false precept,
Of being afore-hand, has deceived a number,
And made them enter quarrels, often-times,
Before they were aware; and afterward,
Against their wills.

    Kas. How must I do then, sir?

    Sub. I cry this lady mercy: she should first
Have been saluted. [*Kisses her.*] I do call you lady,
Because you are to be one, ere 't be long,
My soft and buxom widow.

    Kas. Is she, i'faith?

    Sub. Yes, or my art is an egregious liar.

    Kas. How know you?

    Sub. By inspection on her forehead,
And subtlety of her lip, which must be tasted
Often, to make a judgment. [*Kisses her again.*] 'Slight,
        she melts
Like a myrobolane:—here is yet a line,
In *rivo frontis*, tells me he is no knight.

    Dame P. What is he then, sir?

    Sub. Let me see your hand.
O, your *linea fortunæ* makes it plain;
And stella here *in monte Veneris.*
But, most of all, *junctura annularis.*
He is a soldier, or a man of art, lady,
But shall have some great honour shortly.

    Dame P. Brother,
He's a rare man, believe me!

        Re-enter FACE, *in his uniform.*

    Kas. Hold your peace.
Here comes the t' other rare man.—'Save you, captain.

Face. Good master Kastril! Is this your sister?

Kas. Ay, sir.

Please you to kuss her, and be proud to know her.

Face. I shall be proud to know you, lady. [*Kisses her.*

Dame P. Brother,

He calls me lady too.

Kas. Ay, peace: I heard it.   [*Takes her aside.*

Face. The count is come.

Sub. Where is he?

Face. At the door.

Sub. Why, you must entertain him.

Face. What will you do

With these the while?

Sub. Why, have them up, and shew them

Some fustian book, or the dark glass.

Face. Fore God,

She is a delicate dab-chick! I must have her.   [*Exit.*

Sub. Must you! ay, if your fortune will, you must.—

Come, sir, the captain will come to us presently:

I'll have you to my chamber of demonstrations,

Where I will shew you both the grammar, and logic,

And rhetoric of quarrelling: my whole method

Drawn out in tables; and my instrument,

That hath the several scales upon't, shall make you

Able to quarrel at a straw's-breadth by moonlight.

And, lady, I'll have you look in a glass,

Some half an hour, but to clear your eye-sight,

Against you see your fortune; which is greater,

Than I may judge upon the sudden, trust me.

[*Exit, followed by* KAST. *and* Dame P.

Re-enter FACE.

Face. Where are you, doctor?

Sub. [*within.*] I'll come to you presently.

Face. I will have this same widow, now I have seen her,

On any composition.

Re-enter SUBTLE.

Sub. What do you say?

Face. Have you disposed of them?

Sub. I have sent them up.

Face. Subtle, in troth, I needs must have this widow.

Sub. Is that the matter?

Face. Nay, but hear me.

Sub. Go to,
If you rebel once, Dol shall know it all:
Therefore be quiet, and obey your chance.

Face. Nay, thou art so violent now—Do but conceive....

Sub. I will not treat with thee; what! sell my fortune?
'Tis better than my birth-right. Do not murmur:
Win her, and carry her. If you grumble, Dol
Knows it directly.

Face. Well, sir, I am silent.
Will you go help to fetch in Don in state?   [*Exit.*

Sub. I follow you, sir: we must keep Face in awe,
Or he will over-look us like a tyrant.

Re-enter FACE, *introducing* SURLY *disguised
as a* Spaniard.

Brain of a tailor! who comes here? Don John!

Sur. Señores, beso las manos a vuestras mercedes....

Sub. He looks in that deep ruff like a head in a platter,
Serv'd in by a short cloak upon two trestles.

Face. Or, what do you say to a collar of brawn, cut
down
Beneath the souse, and wriggled with a knife?

Sub. 'Slud, he does look too fat to be a Spaniard.

Face. Perhaps some Fleming or some Hollander got
him
In d' Alva's time; count Egmont's bastard.

Sub. Don,
Your scurvy, yellow, Madrid face is welcome.

Sur. Gratia.

Sub. He speaks out of a fortification.

Pray God he have no squibs in those deep sets.

    Sur. *Por dios, señores, muy linda casa!*

    Sub. What says he?

    Face. Praises the house, I think;
I know no more but's action.

    Sub. Yes, the *casa,*
My precious Diego, will prove fair enough
To cozen you in. Do you mark? you shall
Be cozen'd, Diego.

    Face. Cozen'd, do you see,
My worthy Donzel, cozen'd.

    Sur. *Entiendo.*

    Sub. Do you intend it? so do we, dear Don.
Have you brought pistolets, or portagues,
My solemn Don?—Dost thou feel any?

    Face. [*Feels his pockets.*] Full.

    Sub. You shall be emptied, Don, pumped and drawn
Dry, as they say.

    Face. Milked, in troth, sweet Don.

    Sub. See all the monsters; the great lion of all, Don.

    Sur. *Con licencia, se puede ver a esta señora?*

    Sub. What talks he now?

    Face. Of the sennora.

    Sub. O, Don,
That is the lioness, which you shall see
Also, my Don.

    Face. 'Slid, Subtle, how shall we do?

    Sub. For what?

    Face. Why Dol's employ'd, you know.

    Sub. That's true.
'Fore heaven, I know not: he must stay, that's all.

    Face. Stay! that he must not by no means.

    Sub. No! why?

    Face. Unless you'll mar all. 'Slight, he will suspect it:
And then he will not pay, not half so well....

    Sub. What shall we do then?

    Face. Think: you must be sudden.

    Sur. *Entiendo que la señora es tan hermosa, que codicio
tan verla, como la bien aventuranza de mi vida.*

Face. *Mi vida!* 'Slid, Subtle, he puts me in mind o'
  the widow.
What dost thou say to draw her to it, ha!
And tell her 'tis her fortune? all our venture
Now lies upon't....
What dost thou think on't, Subtle?
  Sub. Who, I? why——
  Face. The credit of our house too is engaged.
  Sub. You made me an offer for my share erewhile.
What wilt thou give me, i' faith?
  Face. O, by that light
I'll not buy now: You know your doom to me.
E'en take your lot, obey your chance, sir; win her,
And wear her out, for me.
  Sub. 'Slight, I'll not work her then.
  Face. It is the common cause; therefore bethink you.
Dol else must know it, as you said.
  Sub. I care not.
  Sur. *Señores, porque se tarda tanto?*
  Sub. Faith, I am not fit, I am old.
  Face. That's now no reason, sir.
  Sur. *Puede ser de hazer burla de mi amor?*
  Face. You hear the Don too? by this air, I call,
And loose the hinges: Dol!
  Sub. A plague of hell——
  Face. Will you then do?
  Sub. You are a terrible rogue!
I'll think of this: will you, sir, call the widow?
  Face. Yes, and I'll take her too with all her faults,
Now I do think on't better.
  Sub. With all my heart, sir;
Am I discharg'd o' the lot?
  Face. As you please.
  Sub. Hands.   *[They take hands.*
  Face. Remember now, that upon any change,
You never claim her.
  Sub. Much good joy, and health to you, sir.
Marry a whore! fate, let me wed a witch first.
  Sur. *Por estas honradas barbas*——

Sub. He swears by his beard.
Dispatch, and call the brother too.   [*Exit* FACE.

Sur. Tengo duda, señores, que no me hagan alguna traycion.

Sub. How, issue on? yes, præsto, sennor. Please you
Enthratha the *chambratha*, worthy don:
Where if you please the fates, in your *bathada*,
You shall be soaked, and stroked, and tubb'd, and rubb'd,
And scrubb'd, and fubb'd, dear don, before you go.
You shall in faith, my scurvy baboon don.
Be curried, claw'd and flaw'd, and taw'd, indeed.
I will the heartlier go about it now,...
To be revenged on this impetuous Face:
The quickly doing of it is the grace.

[*Exeunt* SUB. *and* SURLY.

SCENE II: Another Room in the same.

Enter FACE, KASTRIL, *and* Dame PLIANT.

Face. Come, lady: I knew the doctor would not leave,
Till he had found the very nick of her fortune.

Kas. To be a countess, say you, a Spanish countess,
sir?

Dame P. Why, is that better than an English countess?

Face. Better! 'Slight, make you that a question, lady?

Kas. Nay, she is a fool, captain, you must pardon
her.

Face. Ask from your courtier, to your inns-of-court-
man,
To your mere milliner; they will tell you all,
Your Spanish gennet is the best horse; your Spanish
Stoup is the best garb: your Spanish beard
Is the best cut; your Spanish ruffs are the best
Wear; your Spanish pavin the best dance;
Your Spanish titillation in a glove
The best perfume: and for your Spanish pike,
And Spanish blade, let your poor captain speak—
Here comes the doctor.

Enter SUBTLE, *with a paper.*

Sub. My most honour'd lady,
For so I am now to style you, having found
By this my scheme, you are to undergo
An honourable fortune, very shortly.
What will you say now, if some——
　Face. I have told her all, sir;
And her right worshipful brother here, that she shall be
A countess; do not delay them, sir: a Spanish countess.
　Sub. Still, my scarce-worshipful captain, you can keep
No secret! Well, since he has told you, madam,
Do you forgive him, and I do.
　Kas. She shall do that, sir;
I'll look to't, 'tis my charge.
　Sub. Well then: nought rests
But that she fit her love now to her fortune.
　Dame P. Truly I shall never brook a Spaniard.
　Sub. No!
　Dame P. Never since eighty-eight could I abide them,
And that was some three year afore I was born, in truth.
　Sub. Come, you must love him, or be miserable;
Choose which you will.
　Face. By this good rush, persuade her,
She will cry strawberries else within this twelve-month.
　Sub. Nay, shads and mackerel, which is worse.
　Face. Indeed, sir!
　Kas. 'Ods lid, you shall love him, or I'll kick you.
　Dame P. Why,
I'll do as you will have me, brother.
　Kas. Do,
Or by this hand I'll maul you.
　Face. Nay, good sir,
Be not so fierce.
　Sub. No, my enraged child;
She will be ruled. What, when she comes to taste
The pleasures of a countess! to be courted——
　Face. And kiss'd, and ruffled!
　Sub. Ay, behind the hangings

Face. And then come forth in pomp!...

Sub. Is serv'd
Upon the knee!

Face. And has her pages, ushers,
Footmen, and coaches—

Sub. Her six mares—

Face. Nay, eight!

Sub. To hurry her through London, to the Exchange,
Bethlem, the china-houses—

Face. Yes, and have
The citizens gape at her, and praise her tires,
And my lord's goose-turd bands, that rides with her!

Kas. Most brave! By this hand, you are not my suster,
If you refuse.

Dame P. I will not refuse, brother.

Enter SURLY.

Sur. *Que es esto, señores, que no venga? Esta tardanza
me mata!*

Face. It is the count come:
The doctor knew he would be here, by his art.

Sub. *En gallanta madama, Don! gallantissima!*

Sur. *Por todos los dioses, la mas acabada hermosura,
que he visto en mi vida!*

Face. Is't not a gallant language that they speak?

Kas. An admirable language! Is't not French?

Face. No, Spanish, sir.

Kas. It goes like law French,
And that, they say, is the courtliest language.

Face. List, sir.

Sur. *El sol ha perdido su lumbre, con el esplandor que
trae esta dama! Valgame dios!*

Face. He admires your sister.

Kas. Must not she make curt'sy?

Sub. 'Ods will, she must go to him, man, and kiss
him!
It is the Spanish fashion, for the women
To make first court.

Face. 'Tis true he tells you, sir:

His art knows all.

  Sur. *Porque no se acude?*

  Kas. He speaks to her, I think.

  Face. That he does, sir.

  Sur. *Por el amor de dios, que es esto que se tarda?*

  Kas. Nay, see: she will not understand him! gull,
Noddy.

  Dame P. What say you, brother?

  Kas. Ass, my suster,
Go kuss him, as the cunning man would have you;
I'll thrust a pin in your buttocks else.

  Face. O no, sir.

  Sur. *Señora mia, mi persona esta muy indigna de allegar
a tanta hermosura.*

  Face. Does he not use her bravely?

  Kas. Bravely, i' faith!

  Face. Nay, he will use her better.

  Kas. Do you think so?

  Sur. *Señora, si sera servida, entremonos.*

                            [*Exit with* Dame PLIANT.

  Kas. Where does he carry her?

  Face. Into the garden, sir;
Take you no thought: I must interpret for her.

  Sub. Give Dol the word. [*Aside to* FACE, *who goes
out.*]—Come, my fierce child, advance,
We'll to our quarrelling lesson again.

  Kas. Agreed.
I love a Spanish boy with all my heart.

  Sub. Nay, and by this means, sir, you shall be brother
To a great count.

  Kas. Ay, I knew that at first.
This match will advance the house of the Kastrils.

  Sub. 'Pray God your sister prove but pliant!

  Kas. Why,
Her name is so, by her other husband.

  Sub. How!

  Kas. The widow Pliant. Knew you not that?

  Sub. No faith, sir;
Yet, by erection of her figure, I guest it.

Come, let's go practise.
 Kas. Yes, but do you think, doctor,
I e'er shall quarrel well?
 Sub. I warrant you.   [*Exeunt.*

    SCENE III: Another Room in the same.

 Enter DOL *in her fit of raving, followed by* MAMMON.

 Dol. *For after Alexander's death—*
 Mam. Good lady—
 Dol. *That Perdiccas and Antigonus were slain,*
The two that stood, Seleuc' and Ptolomee—
 Mam. Madam.
 Dol. *Make up the two legs, and the fourth beast,*
That was Gog-north, and Egypt-south: which after
Was call'd Gog-iron-leg, and South-iron-leg—
 Mam. Lady—
 Dol. *And then Gog-horned. So was Egypt, too:*
Then Egypt-clay-leg, and Gog-clay-leg—
 Mam. Sweet madam.
 Dol. *And last Gog-dust, and Egypt-dust, which fall*
In the last link of the fourth chain. And these
Be stars in story, which none see, or look at—
 Mam. What shall I do?
 Dol. *For, as he says, except*
We call the rabbins, and the heathen Greeks—
 Mam. Dear lady.
 Dol. *To come from Salem, and from Athens,*
And teach the people of Great Britain—

   Enter FACE *hastily, in his servant's dress.*

 Face. What's the matter, sir?
 Dol. *To speak the tongue of Eber, and Javan—*
 Mam. O,
She's in her fit.
 Dol. *We shall know nothing——*
 Face. Death, sir,
We are undone!

Dol. *Where then a learned linguist*
Shall see the ancient used communion
Of vowels and consonants——

Face. My master will hear!

Dol. *A wisdom, which Pythagoras held most high——*

Mam. Sweet honourable lady!

Dol. *To comprise*
All sounds of voices, in few marks of letters——

Face. Nay, you must never hope to lay her now.

                                    [*They all speak together.*

Dol. *And so we may arrive by Talmud skill,*
And profane Greek, to raise the building up
Of Helen's house against the Ismaelite,
King of Thogarma, and his habergions
Brimstony, blue, and fiery; and the force
Of king Abaddon, and the beast of Cittim;
Which rabbi David Kimchi, Onkelos,
And Aben Ezra do interpret Rome.

Face. How did you put her into't?

Mam. Alas, I talk'd
Of a fifth monarchy I would erect,
With the philosopher's stone, by chance, and she
Falls on the other four straight.

Face. Out of Broughton!
I told you so. 'Slid, stop her mouth.

Mam. Is't best?

Face. She'll never leave else. If the old man hear her,
We are but fæces, ashes.

Sub. [*within.*] What's to do there?

Face. O, we are lost! Now she hears him, she is quiet.

        Enter SUBTLE, *they run different ways.*

Mam. Where shall I hide me!

Sub. How! what sight is here!
Close deeds of darkness, and that shun the light!
Bring him again. Who is he? What, my son!
O, I have lived too long.

Mam. Nay, good, dear father,
There was no unchaste purpose.

Sub. Not! and flee me,
When I come in?
　Mam. That was my error.
　Sub. Error!
Guilt, guilt, my son: give it the right name. No marvel,
If I found check in our great work within,
When such affairs as these were managing!
　Mam. Why, have you so?
　Sub. It has stood still this half hour:
And all the rest of our less works gone back.
Where is the instrument of wickedness,
My lewd false drudge?
　Mam. Nay, good sir, blame not him;
Believe me, 'twas against his will or knowledge:
I saw her by chance.
　Sub. Will you commit more sin,
To excuse a varlet?
　Mam. By my hope, 'tis true, sir.
　Sub. Nay, then I wonder less, if you, for whom
The blessing was prepared, would so tempt heaven,
And lose your fortunes.
　Mam. Why, sir?
　Sub. This will retard
The work, a month at least.
　Mam. Why, if it do,
What remedy? But think it not, good father:
Our purposes were honest.
　Sub. As they were,
So the reward will prove. [*A loud explosion within.*]—How
　　now! ah me!
God, and all saints be good to us.—

Re-enter FACE.

　　　　　　　　　　　　　What's that?
　Face. O sir, we are defeated! all the works
Are flown *in fumo*, every glass is burst:
Furnace, and all rent down! as if a bolt
Of thunder had been driven through the house.
Retorts, receivers, pelicans, bolt-heads,

All struck in shivers!

> [SUBTLE *falls down as in a swoon.*

Help, good sir! alas,
Coldness, and death invades him. Nay, sir Mammon,
Do the fair offices of a man! you stand,
As you were readier to depart than he.

> [*Knocking within.*

Who's there? my lord her brother is come.

Mam. Ha, Lungs!

Face. His coach is at the door. Avoid his sight,
For he's as furious as his sister's mad.

Mam. Alas!

Face. My brain is quite undone with the fume, sir,
I ne'er must hope to be mine own man again.

Mam. Is all lost, Lungs? will nothing be preserv'd
Of all our cost?

Face. Faith, very little, sir;
A peck of coals or so, which is cold comfort, sir.

Mam. O my voluptuous mind! I am justly punish'd.

Face. And so am I, sir.

Mam. Cast from all my hopes—

Face. Nay, certainties, sir.

Mam. By mine own base affections.

Sub. [*Seeming to come to himself.*] O, the curst fruits of
    vice and lust!

Mam. Good father,
It was my sin. Forgive it.

Sub. Hangs my roof
Over us still, and will not fall, O justice,
Upon us, for this wicked man!

Face. Nay, look, sir,
You grieve him now with staying in his sight:
Good sir, the nobleman will come too, and take you,
And that may breed a tragedy.

Mam. I'll go.

Face. Ay, and repent at home, sir. It may be,
For some good penance you may have it yet;
A hundred pound to the box at Bethlem—

Mam. Yes.

Face. For the restoring such as—have their wits.
Mam. I'll do't.
Face. I'll send one to you to receive it.
Mam. Do.
Is no projection left?
Face. All flown, or stinks, sir.
Mam. Will nought be sav'd that's good for med'cine,
   think'st thou?
Face. I cannot tell, sir. There will be perhaps,
Something about the scraping of the shards,
Will cure the itch,—though not your itch of mind, sir.
                                [*Aside.*
It shall be saved for you, and sent home. Good sir,
This way for fear the lord should meet you.
                        [*Exit* MAMMON.

   Sub. [*raising his head.*] Face!
   Face. Ay.
   Sub. Is he gone?
   Face. Yes, and as heavily
As all the gold he hoped for were in's blood.
Let us be light though.
   Sub. [*leaping up.*] Ay, as balls, and bound
And hit our heads against the roof for joy:
There's so much of our care now cast away.
   Face. Now to our don.
   Sub. Yes, your young widow by this time
Is made a countess, Face; she has been in travail
Of a young heir for you.
   Face. Good, sir.
   Sub. Off with your case,
And greet her kindly, as a bridegroom should,
After these common hazards.
   Face. Very well, sir.
Will you go fetch don Diego off, the while?
   Sub. And fetch him over too, if you'll be pleased, sir:
Would Dol were in her place, to pick his pockets now!
   Face. Why, you can do't as well, if you would set to't.
I pray you prove your virtue.
   Sub. For your sake, sir.   [*Exeunt.*

SCENE IV: Another Room in the same.

Enter SURLY *and* Dame PLIANT.

Sur. Lady, you see into what hands you are fall'n;
'Mongst what a nest of villains! and how near
Your honour was t'have catch'd a certain clap,
Through your credulity, had I but been
So punctually forward, as place, time,
And other circumstances would have made a man;
For you're a handsome woman: would you were wise too!
I am a gentleman come here disguised,
Only to find the knaveries of this citadel;
And where I might have wrong'd your honour, and have
     not,
I claim some interest in your love. You are,
They say, a widow, rich; and I'm a bachelor,
Worth nought: your fortunes may make me a man,
As mine have preserv'd you a woman. Think upon it,
And whether I have deserv'd you or no.
     Dame P. I will, sir.
     Sur. And for these household-rogues, let me alone
To treat with them.

Enter SUBTLE.

Sub. How doth my noble Diego,
And my dear madam countess? hath the count
Been courteous, lady? liberal, and open?
Donzel, methinks you look melancholic,...
I do not like the dulness of your eye;
It hath a heavy cast, 'tis upsee Dutch,
And says you are a lumpish whore-master.
Be lighter, I will make your pockets so.
                              [*Attempts to pick them.*
     Sur. [*Throws open his cloak.*] Will you, don bawd
          and pick-purse? [*strikes him down.*] how now! reel
          you?
Stand up, sir, you shall find, since I am so heavy,
I'll give you equal weight.

Sub. Help! murder!

Sur. No, sir,

There's no such thing intended: a good cart,
And a clean whip shall ease you of that fear.
I am the Spanish don *that should be cozen'd*,
Do you see, cozen'd! Where's your captain Face,
That parcel broker, and whole-bawd, all rascal?

Enter FACE *in his uniform.*

Face. How, Surly!

Sur. O, make your approach, good captain.
I have found from whence your copper rings and spoons
Come, now, wherewith you cheat abroad in taverns.
'Twas here you learn'd t' anoint your boot with brim-
            stone,
Then rub men's gold on't for a kind of touch,
And say 'twas naught, when you had changed the colour,
That you might have't for nothing. And this doctor,
Your sooty, smoky-bearded compeer, he
Will close you so much gold, in a bolt's-head,
And, on a turn, convey in the stead another
With sublimed mercury, that shall burst in the heat,
And fly out all *in fumo!* Then weeps Mammon;
Then swoons his worship. [FACE *slips out.*] Or, he is
            the Faustus,
That casteth figures...
[*Seizes* SUBTLE *as he is retiring.*]—Nay, sir, you must
            tarry,
Though he be scaped; and answer by the ears, sir.

Re-enter FACE *with* KASTRIL.

Face. Why, now's the time, if ever you will quarrel
Well, as they say, and be a true-born child:
The doctor and your sister both are abused.

Kas. Where is he? which is he? he is a slave,
Whate'er he is, and the son of a whore.—Are you
The man, sir, I would know?

Sur. I should be loth, sir,
To confess so much.

Kas. Then you lie in your throat.

Sur. How!

Face. [*to* KASTRIL.] A very errant rogue, sir, and a
cheater,

Employ'd here by another conjurer

That does not love the doctor, and would cross him,

If he knew how.

Sur. Sir, you are abused.

Kas. You lie:

And 'tis no matter.

Face. Well said, sir! He is

The impudent'st rascal——

Sur. You are indeed: Will you hear me, sir?

Face. By no means: bid him be gone.

Kas. Begone, sir, quickly.

Sur. This 's strange!—Lady, do you inform your
brother.

Face. There is not such a foist in all the town,

The doctor had him presently; and finds yet,

The Spanish count will come here.—Bear up, Subtle.

> [*Aside.*

Sub. Yes, sir, he must appear within this hour.

Face. And yet this rogue would come in a disguise,

By the temptation of another spirit,

To trouble our art, though he could not hurt it!

Kas. Ay,

I know—Away, [*to his sister.*] you talk like a foolish
mauther.

Sur. Sir, all is truth she says.

Face. Do not believe him, sir.

He is the lying'st swabber! Come your ways, sir.

Sur. You are valiant out of company!

Kas. Yes, how then, sir?

Enter DRUGGER *with a piece of damask.*

Face. Nay, here's an honest fellow, too, that knows him,

And all his tricks. Make good what I say, Abel,

This cheater would have cozen'd thee o' the widow.—

> [*Aside to* DRUG.

He owes this honest Drugger here seven pound,
He has had on him, in two-penny'orths of tobacco.
   Drug. Yes, sir.
And he has damn'd himself three terms to pay me.
   Face. And what does he owe for lotium?
   Drug. Thirty shillings, sir;
And for six syringes.
   Sur. Hydra of villainy!
   Face. Nay, sir, you must quarrel him out o' the house:
   Kas. I will:
—Sir, if you get not out o' doors, you lie;
And you are a pimp.
   Sur. Why, this is madness, sir,
Not valour in you; I must laugh at this.
   Kas. It is my humour: you are a pimp and a trig,
And an *Amadis de Gaul*, or a Don Quixote.
   Drug. Or a knight o' the curious coxcomb, do you see?

Enter ANANIAS.

   Ana. Peace to the household!
   Kas. I'll keep peace for no man.
   Ana. Casting of dollars is concluded lawful.
   Kas. Is he the constable?
   Sub. Peace, Ananias.
   Face. No, sir.
   Kas. Then you are an otter, and a shad, a whit,
A very tim.
   Sur. You'll hear me, sir?
   Kas. I will not.
   Ana. What is the motive?
   Sub. Zeal in the young gentleman,
Against his Spanish slops.
   Ana. They are profane,
Lewd, superstitious, and idolatrous breeches.
   Sur. New rascals!
   Kas. Will you be gone, sir?
   Ana. Avoid, Sathan!
Thou art not of the light! That ruff of pride
About thy neck, betrays thee; and is the same

With that which the unclean birds, in seventy-seven,
Were seen to prank it with on divers coasts:
Thou look'st like antichrist, in that lewd hat.

   Sur. I must give way.

   Kas. Be gone, sir.

   Sur. But I'll take
A course with you——

   Ana. Depart, proud Spanish fiend!

   Sur. Captain and doctor.

   Ana. Child of perdition!

   Kas. Hence, sir!—   [*Exit* SURLY.
Did I not quarrel bravely?

   Face. Yes, indeed, sir.

   Kas. Nay, an I give my mind to't, I shall do't.

   Face. O, you must follow, sir, and threaten him tame:
He'll turn again else:

   Kas. I'll re-turn him then.   [*Exit.*

           [SUBTLE *takes* ANANIAS *aside.*

   Face. Drugger, this rogue prevented us, for thee:
We had determin'd that thou should'st have come
In a Spanish suit, and have carried her so; and he,
A brokerly slave! goes, puts it on himself.
Hast brought the damask?

   Drug. Yes, sir.

   Face. Thou must borrow
A Spanish suit: hast thou no credit with the players?

   Drug. Yes, sir; did you never see me play the Fool?

   Face. I know not, Nab:—thou shalt, if I can help it.—
           [*Aside.*
Hieronimo's old cloak, ruff, and hat will serve;
I'll tell thee more when thou bring'st 'em.

           [*Exit* DRUGGER.

   Ana. Sir, I know
The Spaniard hates the brethren, and hath spies
Upon their actions: and that this was one
I make no scruple.—But the holy synod
Have been in prayer and meditation for it;
And 'tis reveal'd no less to them than me,
That casting of money is most lawful.

Sub. True,
But here I cannot do it: if the house
Shou'd chance to be suspected, all would out,
And we be lock'd up in the Tower for ever,
To make gold there for the state, never come out;
And then are you defeated.

Ana. I will tell
This to the elders and the weaker brethren,
That the whole company of the separation
May join in humble prayer again.

Sub. And fasting.

Ana. Yea, for some fitter place. The peace of mind
Rest with these walls!   [*Exit.*

Sub. Thanks, courteous Ananias.

Face. What did he come for?

Sub. About casting dollars,
Presently out of hand. And so I told him,
A Spanish minister came here to spy,
Against the faithful—

Face. I conceive. Come, Subtle,
Thou art so down upon the least disaster!
How wouldst thou ha' done, if I had not help't thee
    out?

Sub. I thank thee, Face, for the angry boy, i' faith.

Face. Who would have look'd it should have been
    that rascal?
Surly? he had dyed his beard and all. Well, sir,
Here's damask come to make you a suit.

Sub. Where's Drugger?

Face. He is gone to borrow me a Spanish habit;
I'll be the count, now.

Sub. But where's the widow?

Face. Within, with my lord's sister; madam Dol
Is entertaining her.

Sub. By your favour, Face,
Now she is honest, I will stand again

Face. You will not offer it?

Sub. Why?

Face. Stand to your word,

Or—here comes Dol, she knows—
    Sub. You are tyrannous still.

Enter DOL *hastily.*

    Face. Strict for my right.—How now, Dol! Hast
[thou] told her,
The Spanish count will come?
    Dol. Yes; but another is come,
You little look'd for!
    Face. Who is that?
    Dol. Your master;
The master of the house.
    Sub. How, Dol!
    Face. She lies,
This is some trick. Come, leave your quiblins, Dorothy.
    Dol. Look out, and see.   [FACE *goes to the window.*
    Sub. Art thou in earnest?
    Dol. 'Slight,
Forty o' the neighbours are about him, talking.
    Face. 'Tis he by this good day.
    Dol. 'Twill prove ill day
For some on us.
    Face. We are undone, and taken.
    Dol. Lost, I'm afraid.
    Sub. You said he would not come,
While there died one a week within the liberties.
    Face. No: 'twas within the walls.
    Sub. Was't so! cry you mercy.
I thought the liberties. What shall we do now, Face?
    Face. Be silent: not a word, if he call or knock.
I'll into mine old shape again and meet him,
Of Jeremy, the butler. In the mean time,
Do you two pack up all the goods and purchase,
That we can carry in the two trunks. I'll keep him
Off for to-day, if I cannot longer: and then
At night, I'll ship you both away to Ratcliff,
Where we will meet to-morrow, and there we'll share.
Let Mammon's brass and pewter keep the cellar;
We'll have another time for that. But, Dol,

'Prithee go heat a little water quickly;
Subtle must shave me: all my captain's beard
Must off, to make me appear smooth Jeremy.
You'll do it?

    Sub. Yes, I'll shave you, as well as I can.
    Face. And not cut my throat, but trim me?
    Sub. You shall see, sir.   *[Exeunt.*

ACT THE FIFTH

SCENE I: Before LOVEWIT's door.

Enter LOVEWIT, *with several of the* Neighbours.

Love. Has there been such resort, say you?
1 *Nei.* Daily, sir.
2 *Nei.* And nightly, too.
3 *Nei.* Ay, some as brave as lords.
4 *Nei.* Ladies and gentlewomen.
5 *Nei.* Citizens' wives.
1 *Nei.* And knights.
6 *Nei.* In coaches.
2 *Nei.* Yes, and oyster-women.
1 *Nei.* Beside other gallants.
3 *Nei.* Sailors' wives.
4 *Nei.* Tobacco men.
5 *Nei.* Another Pimlico!
Love. What should my knave advance,
To draw this company? he hung out no banners
Of a strange calf with five legs to be seen,
Or a huge lobster with six claws?
6 *Nei.* No, sir.
3 *Nei.* We had gone in then, sir.
Love. He has no gift
Of teaching in the nose that e'er I knew of.
You saw no bills set up that promised cure
Of agues, or the tooth-ache?
2 *Nei.* No such thing, sir.
Love. Nor heard a drum struck for baboons or
    puppets?
5 *Nei.* Neither, sir.
Love. What device should he bring forth now?
I love a teeming wit as I love my nourishment:
'Pray God he have not kept such open house,
That he hath sold my hangings, and my bedding!

I left him nothing else. If he have eat them,
A plague o' the moth, say I! Sure he has got
Some bawdy pictures to call all this ging;...
Or 't may be, he has the fleas that run at tilt
Upon a table, or some dog to dance.
When saw you him?

   1 *Nei.* Who, sir, Jeremy?

   2 *Nei.* Jeremy butler?

We saw him not this month.

   Love. How!

   4 *Nei.* Not these five weeks, sir.

   6 *Nei.* These six weeks at the least.

   Love. You amaze me, neighbours!

   5 *Nei.* Sure, if your worship know not where he is,
He's slipt away.

   6 *Nei.* Pray god, he be not made away.

   Love. Ha! it's no time to question, then.

                          [Knocks at the door.

   6 *Nei.* About
Some three weeks since, I heard a doleful cry,
As I sat up a mending my wife's stockings.

   Love. 'Tis strange that none will answer! Didst thou
     hear
A cry, sayst thou?

   6 *Nei.* Yes, sir, like unto a man
That had been strangled an hour, and could not speak.

   2 *Nei.* I heard it too, just this day three weeks, at two
     o'clock
Next morning.

   Love. These be miracles, or you make them so!
A man an hour strangled, and could not speak,
And both you heard him cry?

   3 *Nei.* Yes, downward, sir.

   Love. Thou art a wise fellow. Give me thy hand, I pray
     thee,
What trade art thou on?

   3 *Nei.* A smith, an't please your worship.

   Love. A smith! then lend me thy help to get this door
     open.

3 *Nei.* That I will presently, sir, but fetch my tools—
                                                    [*Exit.*
1 *Nei.* Sir, best to knock again, afore you break it.
Love. [*Knocks again.*] I will.

Enter FACE, *in his butler's livery.*

Face. What mean you, sir?
1, 2, 4 *Nei.* O, here's Jeremy!
Face. Good sir, come from the door.
Love. Why, what's the matter?
Face. Yet farther, you are too near yet.
Love. In the name of wonder,
What means the fellow!
Face. The house, sir, has been visited.
Love. What, with the plague? stand thou then farther.
Face. No, sir,
I had it not.
Love. Who had it then? I left
None else but thee in the house.
Face. Yes, sir, my fellow,
The cat that kept the buttery, had it on her
A week before I spied it; but I got her
Convey'd away in the night: and so I shut
The house up for a month—
Love. How!
Face. Purposing then, sir,
T'have burnt rose-vinegar, treacle, and tar,
And have made it sweet, that you shou'd ne'er have
    known it;
Because I knew the news would but afflict you, sir.
Love. Breathe less, and farther off! Why this is
    stranger:
The neighbours tell me all here that the doors
Have still been open—
Face. How, sir!
Love. Gallants, men and women,
And of all sorts, tag-rag, been seen to flock here
In threaves, these ten weeks, as to a second Hogsden,
In days of Pimlico and Eye-bright.

Face. Sir,
Their wisdoms will not say so.
    Love. To-day they speak
Of coaches, and gallants; one in a French hood
Went in, they tell me; and another was seen
In a velvet gown at the window: divers more
Pass in and out.
    Face. They did pass through the doors then,
Or walls, I assure their eye-sights, and their spectacles;
For here, sir, are the keys, and here have been,
In this my pocket, now above twenty days:
And for before, I kept the fort alone there.
But that 'tis yet not deep in the afternoon,
I should believe my neighbours had seen double
Through the black pot, and made these apparitions!
For, on my faith to your worship, for these three weeks
And upwards, the door has not been open'd.
    Love. Strange!
    1 *Nei.* Good faith, I think I saw a coach.
    2 *Nei.* And I too,
I'd have been sworn.
    Love. Do you but think it now?
And but one coach?
    4 *Nei.* We cannot tell, sir: Jeremy
Is a very honest fellow.
    Face. Did you see me at all?
    1 *Nei.* No; that we are sure on.
    2 *Nei.* I'll be sworn o' that.
    Love. Fine rogues to have your testimonies built on!

Re-enter third Neighbour, *with his tools.*

    3 *Nei.* Is Jeremy come!
    1 *Nei.* O, yes; you may leave your tools;
We were deceived, he says.
    2 *Nei.* He has had the keys;
And the door has been shut these three weeks.
    3 *Nei.* Like enough.
    Love. Peace, and get hence, you changelings.

Enter SURLY *and* MAMMON.

Face. Surly come!
And Mammon made acquainted! they'll tell all.
How shall I beat them off? what shall I do?
Nothing's more wretched than a guilty conscience.

                                            [*Aside.*

Sur. No, sir, he was a great physician. This,
It was no bawdy-house, but a mere chancel!
You knew the lord and his sister.

Mam. Nay, good Surly——

Sur. The happy word, BE RICH——

Mam. Play not the tyrant.—

Sur. *Should be to-day pronounced to all your friends.*
And where be your andirons now? and your brass pots,
That should have been golden flaggons, and great
    wedges?

Mam. Let me but breathe. What, they have shut
    their doors,
Methinks!

Sur. Ay, now 'tis holiday with them.

Mam. Rogues,   [*He and* SURLY *knock.*
Cozeners, impostors, bawds!

Face. What mean you, sir?

Mam. To enter if we can.

Face. Another man's house!
Here is the owner, sir: turn you to him,
And speak your business.

Mam. Are you, sir, the owner?

Love. Yes, sir.

Mam. And are those knaves within your cheaters?

Love. What knaves, what cheaters?

Mam. Subtle and his Lungs.

Face. The gentleman is distracted, sir! No lungs,
Nor lights have been seen here these three weeks, sir,
Within these doors, upon my word.

Sur. Your word,
Groom arrogant!

Face. Yes, sir, I am the house-keeper,

And know the keys have not been out of my hands.

    Sur. This is a new Face.

    Face. You do mistake the house, sir:
What sign was't at?

    Sur. You rascal! this is one
Of the confederacy. Come, let's get officers,
And force the door.

    Love. 'Pray you stay, gentlemen.

    Sur. No, sir, we'll come with warrant.

    Mam. Ay, and then
We shall have your doors open. [*Exeunt* MAM. *and* SUR.

    Love. What means this?

    Face. I cannot tell, sir.

    1 *Nei.* These are two of the gallants
That we do think we saw.

    Face. Two of the fools!
You talk as idly as they. Good faith, sir,
I think the moon has crased 'em all.—O me,

Enter KASTRIL.

The angry boy come too! He'll make a noise,
And ne'er away till he have betray'd us all.   [*Aside.*

    Kas. [*knocking.*] What rogues, bawds, slaves, you'll
        open the door, anon!
Punk, cockatrice, my suster! By this light
I'll fetch the marshal to you. You are a whore
To keep your castle——

    Face. Who would you speak with, sir?

    Kas. The bawdy doctor, and the cozening captain,
And puss my suster.

    Love. This is something, sure.

    Face. Upon my trust, the doors were never open, sir.

    Kas. I have heard all their tricks told me twice over,
By the fat knight and the lean gentleman.

    Love. Here comes another.

Enter ANANIAS *and* TRIBULATION.

    Face. Ananias too!
And his pastor!

Tri. [*beating at the door.*] The doors are shut against us.

Ana. Come forth, you seed of sulphur, sons of fire!
Your stench it is broke forth; abomination
Is in the house.

Kas. Ay, my suster's there.

Ana. The place,
It is become a cage of unclean birds.

Kas. Yes, I will fetch the scavenger, and the constable.

Tri. You shall do well.

Ana. We'll join to weed them out.

Kas. You will not come then, punk devise, my sister!

Ana. Call her not sister; she's a harlot verily.

Kas. I'll raise the street.

Love. Good gentleman, a word.

Ana. Satan avoid, and hinder not our zeal!

                              [*Exeunt* ANA., TRIB. *and* KAST.

Love. The world's turn'd Bethlem.

Face. These are all broke loose,
Out of St. Katherine's, where they use to keep
The better sort of mad-folks.

1 Nei. All these persons
We saw go in and out here.

2 Nei. Yes, indeed, sir.

3 Nei. These were the parties.

Face. Peace, you drunkards! Sir,
I wonder at it: please you to give me leave
To touch the door, I'll try an the lock be chang'd.

Love. It mazes me!

Face. [*Goes to the door.*] Good faith, sir, I believe
There's no such thing: 'tis all *deceptio visus.*—
Would I could get him away.   [*Aside.*

Dap. [*within.*] Master captain! master doctor!

Love. Who's that?

Face. Our clerk within, that I forgot! [*Aside.*] I know
    not, sir.

Dap. [*within.*] For God's sake, when will her grace be
    at leisure?

Face. Ha!
Illusions, some spirit o' the air!—His gag is melted,

And now he sets out the throat.   [*Aside.*

    Dap. [*within.*] I am almost stifled——

    Face. Would you were altogether.   [*Aside.*

    Love. 'Tis in the house.

Ha! list.

    Face. Believe it, sir, in the air.

    Love. Peace, you.

    Dap. [*within.*] Mine aunt's grace does not use me well.

    Sub. [*within.*] You fool,

Peace, you'll mar all.

    Face. [*speaks through the key-hole, while* LOVEWIT
      advances to the door unobserved.] Or you will else,
      you rogue.

    Love. O, is it so? then you converse with spirits!—

Come, sir. No more of your tricks, good Jeremy,

The truth, the shortest way.

    Face. Dismiss this rabble, sir.—

What shall I do? I am catch'd.   [*Aside.*

    Love. Good neighbours,

I thank you all. You may depart. [*Exeunt* Neighbours.]

    —Come sir,

You know that I am an indulgent master;

And therefore conceal nothing. What's your medicine,

To draw so many several sorts of wild fowl?

    Face. Sir, you were wont to affect mirth and wit—

But here's no place to talk on't in the street.

Give me but leave to make the best of my fortune,

And only pardon me the abuse of your house:

It's all I beg. I'll help you to a widow,

In recompense, that you shall give me thanks for,

Will make you seven years younger, and a rich one.

'Tis but your putting on a Spanish cloak:

I have her within. You need not fear the house;

It was not visited.

    Love. But by me, who came

Sooner than you expected.

    Face. It is true, sir.

'Pray you forgive me.

    Love. Well: let's see your widow.   [*Exeunt.*

SCENE II: A Room in the same.

Enter SUBTLE, *leading in* DAPPER, *with his eyes bound
as before.*

Sub. How! have you eaten your gag?
Dap. Yes faith, it crumbled
Away in my mouth.
Sub. You have spoil'd all then.
Dap. No!
I hope my aunt of Fairy will forgive me.
Sub. Your aunt's a gracious lady; but in troth
You were to blame.
Dap. The fume did overcome me,
And I did do't to stay my stomach. 'Pray you
So satisfy her grace.

Enter FACE *in his uniform.*
Here comes the captain.
Face. How now! is his mouth down?
Sub. Ay, he has spoken!
Face. A pox, I heard him, and you too.—He's undone
then.—
I have been fain to say, the house is haunted
With spirits, to keep churl back.
Sub. And hast thou done it?
Face. Sure, for this night.
Sub. Why, then triumph and sing
Of Face so famous, the precious king
Of present wits.
Face. Did you not hear the coil
About the door?
Sub. Yes, and I dwindled with it.
Face. Shew him his aunt, and let him be dispatch'd:
I'll send her to you.   [*Exit* FACE.
Sub. Well, sir, your aunt her grace
Will give you audience presently, on my suit,
And the captain's word that you did not eat your gag
In any contempt of her highness.   [*Unbinds his eyes.*
Dap. Not I, in troth, sir.

Enter DOL *like the queen of Fairy.*

Sub. Here she is come. Down o' your knees and
　　wriggle:
She has a stately presence. [DAPPER *kneels, and shuffles*
　　towards her.] Good! Yet nearer,
And bid, God save you!

Dap. Madam!

Sub. And your aunt.

Dap. And my most gracious aunt, God save your grace.

Dol. Nephew, we thought to have been angry with
　　you;
But that sweet face of yours hath turn'd the tide,
And made it flow with joy, that ebb'd of love.
Arise, and touch our velvet gown.

Sub. The skirts,
And kiss 'em. So!

Dol. Let me now stroak that head.
Much, nephew, shalt thou win, much shalt thou spend;
Much shalt thou give away, much shalt thou lend.

Sub. Ay, much! indeed. [*Aside.*] Why do you not
　　thank her grace?

Dap. I cannot speak for joy.

Sub. See, the kind wretch!
Your grace's kinsman right.

Dol. Give me the bird.
Here is your fly in a purse, about your neck, cousin;
Wear it, and feed it about this day sev'n-night,
On your right wrist——

Sub. Open a vein with a pin.
And let it suck but once a week; till then,
You must not look on't.

Dol. No: and, kinsman,
Bear yourself worthy of the blood you come on.

Sub. Her grace would have you eat no more Woolsack
　　pies,
Nor Dagger frumety.

Dol. Nor break his fast
In Heaven and Hell.

   Sub. She's with you every where!
Nor play with costarmongers, at mum-chance, tray-trip,
God make you rich; (when as your aunt has done it;)
But keep
The gallant'st company, and the best games—
   Dap. Yes, sir.
   Sub. Gleek and primero: and what you get, be true
     to us.
   Dap. By this hand, I will.
   Sub. You may bring's a thousand pound
Before to-morrow night, if but three thousand
Be stirring, an you will.
   Dap. I swear I will then.
   Sub. Your fly will learn you all games.
   Face. [*within.*] Have you done there?
   Sub. Your grace will command him no more duties?
   Dol. No:
But come, and see me often. I may chance
To leave him three or four hundred chests of treasure,
And some twelve thousand acres of fairy land,
If he game well and comely with good gamesters.
   Sub. There's a kind aunt!...
But you must sell your forty mark a year, now.
   Dap. Ay, sir, I mean.
   Sub. Or, give 't away; pox on't!
   Dap. I'll give 't mine aunt: I'll go and fetch the
     writings.   [*Exit.*
   Sub. 'Tis well, away.

Re-enter FACE.

   Face. Where's Subtle?
   Sub. Here: what news?
   Face. Drugger is at the door, go take his suit,
And bid him fetch a parson, presently;
Say, he shall marry the widow. Thou shalt spend
A hundred pound by the service! [*Exit* SUBTLE.] Now,
   queen Dol,
Have you pack'd up all?
   Dol. Yes.

Face. And how do you like
The lady Pliant?
  Dol. A good dull innocent.

Re-enter SUBTLE.

  Sub. Here's your Hieronimo's cloak and hat.
  Face. Give me them.
  Sub. And the ruff too?
  Face. Yes; I'll come to you presently.   [*Exit.*
  Sub. Now he is gone about his project, Dol,
I told you of, for the widow.
  Dol. 'Tis direct
Against our articles.
  Sub. Well, we will fit him, wench.
Hast thou gull'd her of her jewels or her bracelets?
  Dol. No; but I will do't.
  Sub. Soon at night, my Dolly,
When we are shipp'd, and all our goods aboard,
Eastward for Ratcliff; we will turn our course
To Brainford, westward, if thou sayst the word,
And take our leaves of this o'er-weening rascal,
This peremptory Face.
  Dol. Content, I'm weary of him.
  Sub. Thou'st cause, when the slave will run a wiving,
     Dol,
Against the instrument that was drawn between us.
  Dol. I'll pluck his bird as bare as I can.
  Sub. Yes, tell her,
She must by any means address some present
To the cunning man, make him amends for wronging
His art with her suspicion; send a ring,
Or chain of pearl; she will be tortured else
Extremely in her sleep, say, and have strange things
Come to her. Wilt thou?
  Dol. Yes.
  Sub. My fine flitter-mouse,
My bird o' the night! we'll tickle it at the Pigeons,
When we have all, and may unlock the trunks,
And say, this's mine, and thine; and thine, and mine.
                                      [*They kiss.*

Re-enter FACE.

Face. What now! a billing?

Sub. Yes, a little exalted

In the good passage of our stock-affairs.

    Face. Drugger has brought his parson; take him in, Subtle,

And send Nab back again to wash his face.

    Sub. I will: and shave himself?   [*Exit.*

    Face. If you can get him.

    Dol. You are hot upon it, Face, whate'er it is!

    Face. A trick that Dol shall spend ten pound a month by.

Re-enter SUBTLE.

Is he gone?

    Sub. The chaplain waits you in the hall, sir.

    Face. I'll go bestow him.   [*Exit.*

    Dol. He'll now marry her, instantly.

    Sub. He cannot yet, he is not ready. Dear Dol,

Cozen her of all thou canst. To deceive him

Is no deceit, but justice, that would break

Such an inextricable tie as ours was.

    Dol. Let me alone to fit him.

Re-enter FACE.

    Face. Come, my venturers,

You have pack'd up all? where be the trunks? bring forth.

    Sub. Here.

    Face. Let us see them. Where's the money?

    Sub. Here,

In this.

    Face. Mammon's ten pound; eight score before:

The brethren's money, this. Drugger's and Dapper's.

What paper's that?

    Dol. The jewel of the waiting maid's,

That stole it from her lady, to know certain——

    Face. If she should have precedence of her mistress?

    Dol. Yes.

    Face. What box is that?

    Sub. The fish-wives' rings, I think,

And the ale-wives' single money: Is't not Dol?

Dol. Yes; and the whistle that the sailor's wife
Brought you to know an her husband were with Ward.

Face. We'll wet it to-morrow; and our silver-beakers
And tavern cups. Where be the French petticoats,
And girdles and hangers?

Sub. Here, in the trunk,
And the bolts of lawn.

Face. Is Drugger's damask there,
And the tobacco?

Sub. Yes.

Face. Give me the keys.

Dol. Why you the keys?

Sub. No matter, Dol; because
We shall not open them before he comes.

Face. 'Tis true, you shall not open them, indeed;
Nor have them forth, do you see? not forth, Dol.

Dol. No!

Face. No, my smock-rampant. The right is, my master
Knows all, has pardon'd me, and he will keep them;
Doctor, 'tis true—you look—for all your figures:
I sent for him, indeed. Wherefore, good partners,
Both he and she be satisfied; for here
Determines the indenture tripartite
'Twixt Subtle, Dol, and Face. All I can do
Is to help you over the wall, o' the back-side,
Or lend you a sheet to save your velvet gown, Dol.
Here will be officers presently, bethink you
Of some course suddenly to 'scape the dock:
For thither you will come else. [*Loud knocking.*] Hark
you, thunder.

Sub. You are a precious fiend!

Offi. [*without.*] Open the door.

Face. Dol, I am sorry for thee i' faith; but hearst thou?
It shall go hard but I will place thee somewhere:
Thou shalt have my letter to mistress Amo—

Dol. Hang you!

Face. Or madam Cæsarean.

Dol. Pox upon you, rogue,

Would I had but time to beat thee!
  Face. Subtle,
Let's know where you set up next; I will send you
A customer now and then, for old acquaintance:
What new course have you?
  Sub. Rogue, I'll hang myself;
That I may walk a greater devil than thou,
And haunt thee in the flock-bed and the buttery.
                                    [*Exeunt.*

SCENE III: An outer Room in the same.

Enter LOVEWIT *in the Spanish dress, with the* Parson.
        [*Loud knocking at the door.*]

  Love. What do you mean, my masters?
  Mam. [*without.*] Open your door,
Cheaters, bawds, conjurers.
  Offi. [*without.*] Or we will break it open.
  Love. What warrant have you?
  Offi. [*without.*] Warrant enough, sir, doubt not,
If you'll not open it.
  Love. Is there an officer, there?
  Offi. [*without.*] Yes, two or three for failing.
  Love. Have but patience,
And I will open it straight.

Enter FACE, *as butler.*

  Face. Sir, have you done?
Is it a marriage? perfect?
  Love. Yes, my brain.
  Face. Off with your ruff and cloak then; be yourself,
    sir.
  Sur. [*without.*] Down with the door.
  Kas. [*without.*] 'Slight, ding it open.
  Love. [*opening the door.*] Hold,
Hold, gentlemen, what means this violence?

MAMMON, SURLY, KASTRIL, ANANIAS,
TRIBULATION, *and* Officers *rush in.*

Mam. Where is this collier?

Sur. And my captain Face?

Mam. These day owls.

Sur. That are birding in men's purses.

Mam. Madam suppository.

Kas. Doxy, my suster.

Ana. Locusts
Of the foul pit.

Tri. Profane as Bel and the dragon.

Ana. Worse than the grasshoppers, or the lice of
Egypt.

Love. Good gentlemen, hear me. Are you officers,
And cannot stay this violence?

1 *Offi.* Keep the peace.

Love. Gentlemen, what is the matter? whom do you
seek?

Mam. The chemical cozener.

Sur. And the captain pander.

Kas. The nun my suster.

Mam. Madam Rabbi.

Ana. Scorpions,
And caterpillars.

Love. Fewer at once, I pray you.

2 *Offi.* One after another, gentlemen, I charge you,
By virtue of my staff.

Ana. They are the vessels
Of pride, lust, and the cart.

Love. Good zeal, lie still
A little while.

Tri. Peace, deacon Ananias.

Love. The house is mine here, and the doors are open;
If there be any such persons as you seek for,
Use your authority, search on o' God's name.
I am but newly come to town, and finding
This tumult 'bout my door, to tell you true,
It somewhat mazed me; till my man, here, fearing

My more displeasure, told me he had done
Somewhat an insolent part, let out my house
(Belike, presuming on my known aversion
From any air o' the town while there was sickness,)
To a doctor and a captain: who, what they are
Or where they be, he knows not.
    Mam. Are they gone?
    Love. You may go in and search, sir. [MAMMON,
    ANA. *and* TRIB. *go in*.] Here, I find
The empty walls worse than I left them, smok'd,
A few crack'd pots, and glasses, and a furnace;
The ceiling fill'd with poesies of the candle...
Only one gentlewoman I met here,
That is within, that said she was a widow——
    Kas. Ay, that's my suster; I'll go thump her. Where
    is she?   [*Goes in*.
    Love. And should have married a Spanish count,
    but he,
When he came to't, neglected her so grossly,
That I, a widower, am gone through with her.
    Sur. How! have I lost her then?
    Love. Were you the don, sir?
Good faith, now, she does blame you extremely, and says
You swore, and told her you had taken the pains
To dye your beard, and umbre o'er your face,
Borrowed a suit, and ruff, all for her love;
And then did nothing. What an oversight,
And want of putting forward, sir, was this!
Well fare an old harquebuzier, yet,
Could prime his powder, and give fire, and hit,
All in a twinkling!

           Re-enter MAMMON.

    Mam. The whole nest are fled!
    Love. What sort of birds were they?
    Mam. A kind of choughs,
Or thievish daws, sir, that have pick'd my purse
Of eight score and ten pounds within these five weeks,
Beside my first materials; and my goods,

That lie in the cellar, which I am glad they have left,
I may have home yet.
   Love. Think you so, sir?
   Mam. Ay.
   Love. By order of law, sir, but not otherwise.
   Mam. Not mine own stuff!
   Love. Sir, I can take no knowledge
That they are yours, but by public means.
If you can bring certificate that you were gull'd of them,
Or any formal writ out of a court,
That you did cozen yourself, I will not hold them.
   Mam. I'll rather lose them.
   Love. That you shall not, sir,
By me, in troth: upon these terms, they are yours.
What, should they have been, sir, turn'd into gold, all?
   Mam. No,
I cannot tell—It may be they should—What then?
   Love. What a great loss in hope have you sustain'd!
   Mam. Not I, the common-wealth has.
   Face. Ay, he would have built
The city new; and made a ditch about it
Of silver, should have run with cream from Hogsden;
That, every Sunday, in Moor-fields, the younkers,
And tits and tom-boys should have fed on, gratis.
   Mam. I will go mount a turnip-cart, and preach
The end of the world, within these two months. Surly,
What! in a dream?
   Sur. Must I needs cheat myself,
With that same foolish vice of honesty!
Come, let us go and hearken out the rogues:
That Face I'll mark for mine, if e'er I meet him.
   Face. If I can hear of him, sir, I'll bring you word,
Unto your lodging; for in troth, they were strangers
To me, I thought them honest as myself, sir.
                    [*Exeunt* MAM. *and* SUR.

         Re-enter ANANIAS *and* TRIBULATION.

   Tri. 'Tis well, the saints shall not lose all yet. Go,
And get some carts——

Love. For what, my zealous friends?

Ana. To bear away the portion of the righteous
Out of this den of thieves.

Love. What is that portion?

Ana. The goods sometimes the orphans', that the brethren
Bought with their silver pence.

Love. What, those in the cellar,
The knight sir Mammon claims?

Ana. I do defy
The wicked Mammon, so do all the brethren,
Thou profane man! I ask thee with what conscience
Thou canst advance that idol against us,
That have the seal? were not the shillings number'd,
That made the pounds; were not the pounds told out,
Upon the second day of the fourth week,
In the eighth month, upon the table dormant,
The year of the last patience of the saints,
Six hundred and ten?

Love. Mine earnest vehement botcher,
And deacon also, I cannot dispute with you:
But if you get you not away the sooner,
I shall confute you with a cudgel.

Ana. Sir!

Tri. Be patient, Ananias.

Ana. I am strong,
And will stand up, well girt, against an host,
That threaten Gad in exile.

Love. I shall send you
To Amsterdam, to your cellar.

Ana. I will pray there,
Against thy house: may dogs defile thy walls,
And wasps and hornets breed beneath thy roof,
This seat of falsehood, and this cave of cozenage!

[Exeunt ANA. *and* TRIB.

Enter DRUGGER.

Love. Another too?

Drug Not I, sir, I am no brother.

K   8

Love. [*beats him.*] Away, you Harry Nicholas! do you
  talk?
                                          [*Exit* DRUG.
Face. No, this was Abel Drugger. Good sir, go,
                                       [*To the* Parson.
And satisfy him; tell him all is done:
He staid too long a washing of his face.
The doctor, he shall hear of him at West-chester;
And of the captain, tell him, at Yarmouth, or
Some good port-town else, lying for a wind.
                                          [*Exit* Parson.
If you can get off the angry child, now, sir—

              Enter KASTRIL *dragging in his sister.*

Kas. Come on, you ewe, you have match'd most
    sweetly, have you not?...
'Slight, you are a mammet! O, I could touse you, now.
Death, mun' you marry, with a pox!
  Love. You lie, boy...
  Kas. Anon!
  Love. Come, will you quarrel? I will feize you, sirrah;
Why do you not buckle to your tools?
  Kas. 'Od's light,
This is a fine old boy as e'er I saw!
  Love. What, do you change your copy now? proceed,
Here stands my dove: stoop at her, if you dare.
  Kas. 'Slight, I must love him! I cannot choose,
    i' faith,
An I should be hang'd for't! Suster, I protest,
I honour thee for this match.
  Love. O, do you so, sir?
  Kas. Yes, an thou canst take tobacco and drink, old
    boy,
I'll give her five hundred pound more to her marriage,
Than her own state.
  Love. Fill a pipe full, Jeremy.
  Face. Yes; but go in and take it, sir.
  Love. We will—
I will be ruled by thee in anything, Jeremy.

Kas. 'Slight, thou art not hide-bound, thou art a jovy
       boy!
Come, let us in, I pray thee, and take our whiffs.
   Love. Whiff in with your sister, brother boy. [*Exeunt*
KAS. *and* Dame P.] That master
That had received such happiness by a servant,
In such a widow, and with so much wealth,
Were very ungrateful, if he would not be
A little indulgent to that servant's wit,
And help his fortune, though with some small strain
Of his own candour. [*advancing.*]—*Therefore, gentlemen,*
And kind spectators, if I have outstript
An old man's gravity, or strict canon, think
What a young wife and a good brain may do;
Stretch age's truth sometimes, and crack it too.
Speak for thyself, knave.
   Face. *So I will, sir.* [advancing to the front of the
       stage.] *Gentlemen,*
My part a little fell in this last scene,
Yet 'twas decorum. And though I am clean
Got off from Subtle, Surly, Mammon, Dol,
Hot Ananias, Dapper, Drugger, all
With whom I traded; yet I put myself
On you, that are my country: and this pelf,
Which I have got, if you do quit me, rests
To feast you often, and invite new guests.   [Exeunt.

pay ear-rent, i.e. lose your ears [in the pillory].

don Provost, a city officer similar to our Commissioner of Police.

9 **crewel,** yarn. Note the pun on crewel and cruel and on the two meanings of *worsted*. Cf. *King Lear*, where the Fool says: "Ha! ha! look—he wears cruel garters."

Claridiana, the heroine of a romance of chivalry called the *Mirror of Knighthood*, a translation of one of the Spanish cycle of romances. Cf. also Amadis de Gaul (p. 90 and note).

quodling, codling, an unripe apple; came to be used for a 'green' youth.

the Dagger, a gambling house.

familiar, an attendant spirit; **rifle,** raffle, play at dice.

10 **Read,** apparently the Professor of Physic of this name who was charged with practising astrology in 1608.

11 **court-hand,** the style of handwriting used in the law courts until the reign of George II.

chiaus, a Turkish messenger or envoy. Apparently, though the story has no historical authority, the word came to signify a swindler because of one notorious chiaus who defrauded London merchants of a large sum of money in 1609.

a horse draw you, i.e. in a cart to the gallows.

fly, an attendant demon, from the idea that devils were supposed to assume the form of flies.

Clim o' the Cloughs, or Claribels, heroes of old ballads and romances.

five-and-fifty, and flush, terms from an old card game called Primero; apparently synonymous with a very good hand. A clever player would not betray by his face that he had good cards (*spit out secrets like hot custard*).

12 **puckfist,** a close-fisted or niggardly person.

13 **bird,** familiar spirit.

not a mouth shall eat for him, etc. On the strength of his winnings his gambling friends will get their meals at the ordinaries 'on credit' (*on the score*).

14 **dead Holland, living Isaac,** presumably well-known gamblers of the time.

six of your gallants to a cloak, win everything from them except their cloaks, which they would keep to cover the loss of the rest.

15 cawl, membrane.

I'fac, a corruption of 'in faith.'

16 good wives, addressed to some women waiting within.

17 free of the grocers, a member of the Grocers' Company.

if I do see them, a play on the two meanings of *angel*, an attendant spirit and a coin.

sophisticate, adulterate.

grains, spices.

18 maple block, etc. Tobacconists did not merely sell tobacco, but provided conveniences for smoking it, such as a block to cut the tobacco on and tongs to hold the coal.

goldsmith. Goldsmiths were also money-lenders.

of the clothing of his company, a liveryman of the Grocers' Company.

call'd to the scarlet, made a sheriff.

fine for't, pay the fine for declining the office.

amused, amazed.

metoposcopy, reading character from the face.

horoscope, house, see note on p. 6, *searching for things lost.*

Ormus, or Hormuz, on the Persian Gulf.

19 seem to, deem it seemly to.

vice, machinery of wires to move the puppet.

fucus, cosmetic.

portague, gold coin worth about £3. 12s.

20 beech-coal. What its peculiar properties were is not known, but it was evidently essential in alchemy. See also p. 25, last line; and cf. Chaucer, *Canon's Yeoman's Tale*, l. 375, where one of the causes of the Canon's failure to produce gold is said to be: "By-cause our fyr ne was nat maad of beech."

crosslet, crucible; **cucurbite,** gourd-shaped vessel.

21 trunk, speaking-tube.

reaching his dose, offering his remedy.

pomander, a perfume, supposed to keep off the plague.

elixir, i.e. the philosopher's stone.

ACT II, SCENE I

22 hollow dye, dice hollowed out and then loaded so that they fall as desired.

be at charge...young heir. This alludes to the 'commodity' swindle, a well-known practice among usurers at the time. The borrower was compelled to take the whole or part of the loan in goods and to raise what he could by reselling them, probably to the usurer himself. Surly seems to have kept a special retainer whose business it was to make the borrower sign (*seal*) the mortgage.

entrails, linings.

madam Augusta's, a gambling den.

sons of Sword and Hazard, i.e. those who make a living by gambling.

fire-drake, Lungs, an alchemist's assistant, whose business was chiefly to look after the fire. Cf. Chaucer, *Canon's Yeoman's Tale*, l. 200: "I blowe the fyr til that myn herte feynte."

firk up, arouse.

faithful, believing.

23 Lothbury, a street near the Bank of England, at that time inhabited by founders.

make them perfect Indies, change their tin to gold.

Venus, copper; **moon** and **sun,** silver and gold (cf. *Sol* and *Luna* above, and Introduction).

24 the players. The theatres, which were closed during the plague, would be re-opened and the actors would thank Mammon for restoring their means of livelihood.

he that built the Water-work. Jonson is probably referring to the water-works built some fifteen years previously by Bevis Bulmer, for distributing Thames water.

I have a piece of Jason's fleece, etc. References to the association of mythology and alchemy and to the explanation of Greek mythological characters as symbolical of astrological terms are to be found in other writers also.

argent-vive, mercury.

25 alembic, the cap of the distilling apparatus; hence likened to a helmet.

Jove's shower, an allusion to the Danäe myth.

Demogorgon, a demon mentioned by the fourteenth-century Italian writer Boccaccio in his *Decameron*.

crimson, see note on *several colours* below.

bolt's-head, a glass vessel with a long neck.

shingles, wooden house-tiles.

complexion. Chaucer also mentions the effect of the heat and the fumes on the complexion and the eyes: *Canon's Yeoman's Tale,* ll. 174-5:

> "And wher my colour was bothe fresh and reed,
> Now is it wan and of a leden hewe."

26 **several colours.** An allusion to the various colours (each symbolised by a bird or animal) assumed by the materials during the processes of alchemy, the red being the final stage.

seraglio, harem.

Elephantis, a licentious Greek poet, whose works the Emperor Tiberius is said to have had in his villa at Capreae.

Aretine, Pietro Aretino, a licentious Italian satirist of the sixteenth century, noted chiefly for sonnets engraved on a series of statues.

Apicius, a Roman glutton who lived in the reigns of Augustus and Tiberius.

calver'd, cooked in a certain way.

knots, birds of the snipe family.

27 **barbel,** mullet.

prevent, anticipate.

28 **medicine of the triple soul,** i.e. the philosopher's stone, which was regarded as containing the three elements of nature: animal, vegetable and mineral.

Ulen Spiegel, the peasant hero of an early German jest-book, the counterpart of our English Robin Goodfellow and Robin Hood.

register, a plate for regulating the draught in a furnace and so controlling the heat.

aludels, vessels of earthenware or glass.

on D. There are evidently several furnaces, each distinguished by a letter.

29 gripe's egg, a vessel shaped like a large bird's (possibly an ostrich's) egg.

lute, cover with mud or clay, to seal the vessel or protect it from fire.

balneo, short for balneo Mariae, or S. Mary's bath, a vessel of hot water, in which other vessels were put to warm.

canting, the secret language of professional beggars, thieves, etc.

philosopher's wheel. What this means is not known, except that it represents a stage in the process, directions for which were perhaps tabulated in a circular diagram.

lent, slow; **Athanor,** a digesting furnace, digestion in alchemy being the process of separating the various components of a substance.

imbibition, saturation in liquid.

helm, see note on p. 25, *alembic*.

lac virginis (or *philosopher's vinegar*), mercury, supposed by alchemists to be present in all metals.

30 reverberate. A reverberating furnace was one in which reflected, as opposed to direct, heat was used.

crow's head, see note on p. 26, *several colours*.

hay, a net for catching rabbits. Surly continues his rabbit-catching metaphor in his next two speeches.

nipp'd to digestion, with the neck pinched together and so sealed preparatory to being put in the digesting furnace.

Mars, iron.

pellican, a glass vessel.

sign'd with Hermes' seal, i.e. hermetically sealed.

white shirt on, i.e. has reached the white stage.

inceration, the process of reducing to a wax-like consistency.

31 fixation, solidification.

ascension, evaporation.

kemia, a distilling vessel.

34 marchesite, any stone containing metal.

tutie, an oxide of zinc which adheres to the chimneys of furnaces in which brass is melted.

adrop, another synonym for the philosopher's stone.

lato, a yellow metal; **azoch,** mercury; **zernich,** a yellow pigment; **chibrit,** sulphur; **heautarit,** meaning unknown. **merd,** filth.

35 **I warrant thee,** i.e. I will protect you from Subtle's anger.

Bradamante, heroine in the Italian poet Ariosto's *Orlando Furioso.*

Paracelsian, i.e. a follower of Paracelsus (1490–1541), the famous Swiss physician and chemist who advocated mineral remedies for diseases, as opposed to **Galen** (second century A.D.) who advocated vegetable remedies. The regular physicians of Jonson's time were Galenists.

36 **Broughton,** Hugh Broughton (1549–1612), a Hebrew scholar and author of the *Concent of Scripture,* in which he attempted to settle Biblical chronology.

37 **lunary,** a plant used by alchemists.

primero, gleek, card games (see note on p. 11).

lutum, mud or clay, see note on p. 29, *lute;* **menstruum,** see note on p. 7.

38 **by attorney,** not in his own person, i.e. disguised; **a second purpose,** i.e. other than that intended by Face.

find, i.e. be involved in.

parlous, perilous, shrewd.

Bantam, a rich city in Java, synonymous with wealth.

39 **statelich,** a corruption of German.

40 **gold-end-man,** one who buys odds and ends of gold.

discipline, the word by which the ecclesiastical polity of the Puritan party was denoted. The Puritans came, thence, to be styled 'Disciplinarians.'

phlegma, a liquid obtained from vegetable matter.

Lullianist, a disciple of Raymond Lully (1235–1315), a famous Spanish missionary and alchemist.

Ripley, a writer on alchemy, who first introduced Lully's writings into this country. Died about 1490.

sublime, refine; **dulcify,** remove the acids out of a substance; **calcine,** reduce by heat to a calx or powder.

sapor. There were said to be nine sapors, or tastes, in alchemy, of which these are two: the sour taste (*pontic*) and the less sour (*stiptic*, astringent). Each indicated a particular stage in the process of transmuting metals.

41 **Knipper-doling** was a fanatical anabaptist of Münster in Germany. He was associated in the socialistic crusade in that town in 1534.

chrysopœia, spagyrica, synonyms for alchemy.

pamphysic, panarchic, words coined by Subtle, to impress Ananias.

cohobation, a form of distillation.

vivification (the opposite of *mortification*), the restoring of a chemical or metal to its natural form, e.g. from a solution to a solid.

aqua regis, a mixture of acids, so called because it can dissolve gold.

trine circle, astrological jargon.

proper passion, peculiar passive quality.

antimony renders gold less malleable, when alloyed with it.

suscitability, excitability.

magisterium, meaning, not, as above (p. 21), the philosopher's stone itself, but the operations conducted by the alchemist.

43 **pin-dust,** metal filings produced in the manufacture of pins.

Piger Henricus, lit. lazy Henry: a furnace which fed other furnaces and so saved labour.

sericon and bufo, chemical ingredients of alchemy.

44 **Baiards,** Bayard was the name of a magic horse which figures in the legends of Charlemagne. Thence it came to be used proverbially to denote blindness both physical and intellectual: Chaucer, *Canon's Yeoman's Tale*, l. 860: "as bolde as is Bayard the blinde."

Dee, an allusion to John Dee (see Introd.).

leg, bow.

45 **bona roba,** handsome woman.

a cop, on top [of her head]. Perhaps the fashion was to wear hoods tilted to one side.

ACT III, Scene I

48 saints. Such words as *saints, separation, zeal, heathen, Canaan,* were common in the vocabulary of the Puritans of the period, whom Jonson bitterly satirises in the characters of Wholesome and Ananias (see Introd.).

49 aurum potabile, i.e. bribery. Jonson is also alluding to a notorious quack of the time, Francis Anthony, who claimed to cure all diseases by a remedy which he called *aurum potabile.* He was repeatedly imprisoned for practising without a license from the College of Physicians, but his son, none the less, kept on the right side of the law and succeeded to his father's practice.

edified, been instructed.

ACT III, Scene II

furnus acediæ, see note on p. 43, *Piger Henricus.*

turris circulatorius, a distilling vessel.

50 fricace, friction, rubbing.

Christ-tide, the Puritans avoided the use of the Popish word 'mass.'

parcel, partly.

51 no, nor your holy vizard.... In this and the next speech of Subtle's Jonson enumerates the common charges against the Puritans.

52 shorten so your ears, i.e. lose them in the pillory.

wood, a crowd.

I hate traditions. Religious traditions were not accepted by the Puritans; they held the Bible to be the only true basis of faith and conduct.

53 potate, liquefied.

citronise, become yellow.

fimus equinus, see note on p. 5, *clibanum*; **balnei,** see note on p. 29.

54 no magistrate. The Puritans were said to recognise no civil form of government, the Bible being their only code.

the round. The Temple Church is a round church.

55 slops, large trousers, as worn by seamen.

hoys, small sailing vessels; **trunks,** trunk-hose.

John Leydens. Wholesome and Ananias are so called presumably because Leyden was a place to which large numbers of Puritans fled for refuge.

56 **adalantado** (Spanish), meaning strictly a governor of a province.

Verdugo (Spanish), hangman.

58 **angry boys,** a set of riotous youths, common in the time of Elizabeth and James I; they usually went under the title of 'Roaring Boys.'

tobacco. At Drugger's shop these young men would learn and practise the smart ways of smoking.

the duello. The whole of this speech is a satire on the ridiculous pitch of *finesse* to which duelling and quarrelling had been brought (cf. Act IV, Scene I, pp. 72–74). In *As You Like It*, Act V, Sc. 4, Touchstone catalogues the various degrees of the lie: "O sir, we quarrel in print—by the book: as you have books for good manners. I will name you the degrees. The first, the Retort Courteous; the second, the Quip Modest; the third, the Reply Churlish; the fourth, the Reproof Valiant; the fifth, the Countercheck Quarrelsome; the sixth, the Lie with Circumstance; the seventh, the Lie Direct. All these you may avoid, but the Lie Direct."

in diameter, i.e. the lie direct, as opposed to the lie circumstantial.

59 **groom porter,** an official of the Royal household, whose chief function was to supervise all matters connected with gaming within the Court.

ordinaries bid for him. The proprietors of eating-houses would offer free entertainment to fashionable and successful gamblers, as a draw to others. See also note on p. 13, *not a mouth....*

60 **cast,** cashiered.

by most swift posts, as quickly as by the fastest post-horses.

vacation, see note on p. 7, *term.*

commodity, another allusion to the 'commodity' swindle. See note on p. 22, *be at charge....*

61 **Sea-coal-lane,** a lane near Fleet Street, no longer existing.

pellitory, a small plant growing on walls.

water-work, see note on p. 24.

62 **Harry's sovereign,** i.e. of Henry VII or Henry VIII.

groat =fourpence.

noble, an old English coin worth 6*s.* 8*d.* The miscellaneous coins enumerated by Dapper do not total twenty nobles (£6. 13*s.* 4*d.*) unless for some reason the Harry's sovereign was only worth 10*s.*

Philip and Maries, coins with the heads of Philip and Mary facing each other, Philip of Spain being nominally associated with his wife in the throne of England.

63 **spur-ryal,** a gold coin worth about 15*s.*, so called from the resemblance of the sun on the reverse side to the rowel of a spur.

64 **his suit,** i.e. Face's.

65 **crincle,** shrink from one's purpose.

ACT IV, Scene I

68 **Austriac princes.** The house of Austria were supposed to have remarkable lower lips.

69 **Kelly.** See Introduction. The emperor with whom he had dealings was Rudolph II of Germany.

adamant. The pun would be more noticeable with the old spelling of *diamond*, diamant.

70 **mastery** (*magisterium* elsewhere), the philosopher's stone or the operations which produce it.

71 **rabins,** rabbis.

72 **terræ fili,** meaning, besides 'boy of land,' a person of low origin, a son of the earth.

grammar, logic, etc. Subtle introduces terms from logic and philosophy to confuse Kastril.

73 **myrobolane,** some kind of dried fruit, used as a sweetmeat.

rivo frontis, a term from the 'science' of metoposcopy (cf. note on p. 18); probably taken from the book on the subject by Cardano, a famous Italian physician (1501–76).

74 **fustian book,** i.e. a book full of incomprehensible jargon.

75 Don John. Don John of Austria, who commanded the
fleets of Spain and Venice, and won a great victory, at
Lepanto in 1571. He was publicly adopted by Philip II
of Spain as a member of the Royal Family, and was con-
sidered the type of the Spanish nobleman.

souse, ear.

wriggled, i.e. cut round the edge so as to look like the
folds of a ruff.

d'Alva, Fernando Alvarez, Duke of Alva (1508–82),
governor of the Netherlands from 1567–73.

Egmont, Lamoral, Count of Egmont (1522–68), a Flemish
patriot put to death by Alva.

76 sets, folds of a ruff.

Diego, the Spanish equivalent of the Christian name James,
used as a name for any Spaniard.

Donzel, a young Spaniard not yet knighted, the diminutive
of Don.

pistolet, or pistole, a Spanish gold coin worth about 16s. 8d.

77 your doom to me, i.e. Subtle's recent threat to inform Dol.

78 fub, to cheat.

flaw, to crack; **taw,** to prepare raw material, especially
hides, and so used figuratively like our slang word 'tan.'

ACT IV, SCENE II

stoup, some Spanish mode of deportment, such as a bow;
garb was not confined to dress, but could mean a 'fashion'
of any kind. James I cultivated the friendship of Spain
and accordingly Spanish fashions prevailed at Court, though
not among the people (see Dame Pliant's remark below:
"Never since eighty-eight, could I abide them").

pavin, a majestic dance; derived from the Latin *pavo,* a
peacock.

79 scheme, in astrology, a horoscope.

eighty-eight, 1588, the year of the Armada.

rush, the rushes strewn on the floor.

80 the Exchange, *The Royal Exchange* opened by Queen
Elizabeth in 1571; it contained shops and was generally
a place of resort.

Bethlem, the Bethlehem Hospital for the insane, where the lunatics could be viewed on payment of a small fee.

china-houses, i.e. where china could be seen exhibited. Chinese ware had not long been imported and was still an object of novelty.

bands, neck-bands or collar, in this case of the colour of goose-dung (cf. the French *merde d'oie*, gosling green).

law French. A sort of French was used in the law courts, dating from the Norman Conquest.

81 **the word,** i.e. to begin her fit of raving.

erection of her figure, a pun on two meanings: 'her appearance' and 'her horoscope'; see note on p. 6, *searching for things lost.*

ACT IV, Scene III

82 **Perdiccas,** assassinated in Egypt in 321 B.C., and Antigonus, slain in the battle of Ipsus, 301 B.C., were with Seleukus and Ptolemy the four chief generals of Alexander the Great. The use of ancient history in the interpretation of *Revelation* and other parts of the Bible is still common.

as he says, i.e. Broughton; see note on p. 36.

Eber, Heber, great-grandson of Shem, ancestor of the Hebrews.

Javan, son of Japheth, here presumably represented as ancestor of the Greeks.

83 **vowels and consonants,** Broughton believed in the inspiration of the actual text of the Bible.

Thogarma. The kingdom of Togarmah is mentioned in *Ezekiel*, xxvii. 14 and xxxviii. 6, and is usually supposed to be Armenia.

habergions, coats of mail armour, here used to denote the wearers.

Helen, Abaddon, Cittim. These names, and most of Dol's previous raving, are to be found scattered in Broughton's works. Abaddon occurs in *Revelation* ix. 11: "the angel of the bottomless pit...is Abaddon."

David Kimchi, jewish grammarian and Biblical scholar (1160–1232).

Onkelos, one of the targumists, or translators of certain parts of the Old Testament into Chaldee.

Aben Ezra (1092–1167), a wandering Hebrew writer and Biblical critic, the 'Rabbi Ben Ezra' of Browning.

fifth monarchy. A sect which called itself 'Fifth Monarchy Men' and believed that the Millennium was near at hand, when Christ would come and establish the fifth monarchy, was prominent in Cromwell's time. The four previous 'monarchies' were those of Assyria, Persia, Greece and Rome.

86 **have their wits,** i.e. even the inmates of Bethlehem Hospital for the insane are sane in comparison with Mammon.

your case, his uniform as Lungs. He deals with Dame Pliant as Capt. Face.

ACT IV, Scene IV

87 **clap,** mishap.

'tis upsee Dutch, i.e. it is the eye of a Dutchman who is drunk. The word *upsee* (from the Dutch), meaning 'after the manner of,' was used in such phrases as 'upsee Friese,' 'upsee Dutch,' 'upsee English,' all of them suggestive of heavy drinking.

88 **cart,** see note on p. 8, *ride*.

parcel, partly; **broker,** go-between in love affairs.

89 **foist,** cheat.

mauther, girl.

90 **Hydra,** the number of 'heads' against him makes this a suitable simile.

trig, dandy.

Amadis de Gaul, the hero of the oldest cycle of romances of the days of chivalry, similar to our English Sir Galahad.

whit, tim, terms of personal abuse.

91 **in seventy-seven.** The event of the year 1577 alluded to was probably of no more than topical interest and cannot be traced.

Hieronimo, the hero of *The Spanish Tragedy*, by Thomas Kyd (1558–1594), the most popular play of Jonson's youth.

93 **liberties,** the districts of a city which lay beyond the control of the municipal authorities, i.e. the slums.

purchase, stolen goods.

Ratcliff, a village on the Thames near Limehouse.

ACT V, SCENE I

95 **Pimlico,** not the modern district of that name; it was near Hoxton and was a great summer resort.

teaching in the nose, i.e. preaching like a Puritan, with a nasal delivery.

96 **downward,** evidently used in some sense which implies scepticism, like our slang phrase, 'over the left.'

97 **threaves,** hordes.

Hogsden, Hoxton, which was at this time mostly open fields, to which Londoners came on holidays.

Eye-bright, a kind of ale.

98 **in a French hood,** i.e. Dame Pliant.

99 **a great physician,** cf. Act II, Sc. I, p. 35.

mere, absolute.

Be rich, cf. Act II, Sc. I, p. 22.

ACT V, SCENE II

103 **coil,** tumult.

104 **Woolsack,** an Aldgate tavern, disreputable but famous for its pies.

Dagger frumety, see note on p. 9. *Frumety*, or frumenty, was a dish made of wheat boiled in milk and seasoned with sugar, cinnamon, etc. The word is found in Thomas Hardy's novels.

Heaven and Hell were two alehouses near Westminster Hall. Pepys dined at Heaven on 28 January, 1660.

105 **mum-chance, tray-trip, God make you rich,** games of chance, the first two probably played with dice.

when as, when.

gleek and primero (see notes on pp. 11 and 37) were played at Court.

106 Brainford, Brentford, some 6 or 8 miles from London.

the Pigeons, 'The Three Pigeons' at Brentford.

108 single money, small change.

Ward, a famous pirate.

hanger, the strap on which the sword was hung from the sword-belt; often richly ornamented.

bolts, rolls.

smock, a woman's garment, here used to denote the woman herself.

you look, you are surprised.

mistress Amo,...madam Cæsarean, keepers of gambling dens.

ACT V, Scene III

109 for failing, for fear of failing.

ding, break.

110 Bel and the dragon. An allusion to the book of this name in the *Apocrypha*.

caterpillars, a current term for rogues and thieves.

cart, see note on p. 8, *ride*.

112 younkers, youngsters.

tit, girl.

cheat myself, i.e. of the widow.

hearken out, search out by inquiry.

113 that have the seal, that are sealed as God's people. Cf. *Revelation* ix. 4: "those men which have not the seal of God in their foreheads."

table dormant, a table fixed to the floor.

patience, suffering.

Amsterdam, where Tribulation is pastor.

114 Harry Nicholas was a religious enthusiast of the latter half of the sixteenth century, who founded on the Continent a religious sect called 'The Family of Love.'

West-chester, Chester, a convenient point of departure for Ireland, and consequently a resort for fugitives from justice.

mammet, puppet.

touse, tear, pull about.

feize, drive, flog.

stoop, a term from falconry, meaning to pounce upon as a hawk does. It is, thus, a pun on the name Kastril (kestrel).

115 **candour,** good reputation.

'twas decorum, it was all of a part with my character.

country, in a legal sense, meaning a 'jury.'